THE SPRING OF '31

A Kid's View of the Great Depression

By

James E. Munden, Sr.

This book is a work of non-fiction. Some names and places have been changed to protect the privacy of all individuals. The events and situations are true.

ISBN: 1-4140-3512-8 (e-book)
ISBN: 1-4140-3511-X (Paperback)

Library of Congress Control Number: 2003098987

This book is printed on acid free paper.

Printed in the United States of America
Bloomington, IN

Editor: Genevieve Munden

1stBooks - rev. 02/11/04

The Spring of '31

A Kid's View of
The Great Depression

James E. Munden, Sr.

Acknowledgments

This story is written in fond memory of my grandparents, Isaac and Ophelia Munden; Otho and Ila Munden, my father and mother who worked and played with us kids every step of the way; and brother Bill (Braxton), who passed away at too young an age.

Best wishes to his wife, Dell, their children, Terri and Jerry, and their families. Bill loved you all.

To sister, Julie, and brother, Tom: It has been a mental strain trying to recall all we did 75 years ago, but, believe me, I do remember it all. And it was just about all good. And it has been especially good through the decades, as our families have had a close relationship and many laughs together. Thanks for your inspiration.

Many thanks to my wife, Jane, and son, James, Jr. for their encouragement and suggestions, and to daughter, Genevieve for her boundless energy and time spent scanning photos, editing contents and helping format this book. They are the light of my life and all of them express their love for Dad. And I wouldn't have known any of them had I remained in the Navy in 1946.

I hope that this recollection will be an insight into the past for interested family members, presently, and even an eon or two in the future.

Table Of Contents

Preface

In Flanders Field
The poppies grow,
Between the crosses,
Row on row,
That mark our places.

...A sad line from a World War I poem by John McRae, which made a strong impression on me in school in the early 1930's, as did the huge forlorn statue of a doughboy soldier, which still stands on the courthouse square of Smithfield, NC three generations later.

My first trip to town from my grandparents' farm 5 miles away, where we lived, was probably during 1927 or '28 when I was 3 or 4 years old, and that statue made an indelible imprint on me, and I still think about it in 2002 when I pass through Smithfield.

No one living in the '30's would have believed that the world could erupt into war again and destroy many of our generation by the time I turned twenty-one in 1945. The town didn't erect another statue for my schoolmates who didn't come back from WWII and I am glad they didn't... But the doughboy still guards the square, a relic of an older folly.

O'er Omaha Beach,
The lilies grow,
Among the crosses,
Row on row...

So, my reflections are of that time between the two great wars - how things were in the isolated farm community where I was born in 1924, the economic debacle, which brought hardship to our country and the world in the 1930's, and growing up face-to-face with WWII.

The Early Days

Smithfield, situated on the Neuse River in Johnston County between Raleigh and Goldsboro, was already 150 years old, having been incorporated in 1777 during the Revolutionary war when North Carolina was still a colony of Great Britain. The major railroads of the 1800's, north/south and east/west, bypassed the town by a few miles and this stifled its growth as transportation routes foretold the economic future of the area. Smithfield has always been a spicy and classy little town, much good, but a lot of it downright bad. It has a history.

Around 1771 Gov. Tryon, our colonial governor, assembled Royal troops at Smith's Ferry, (Smithfield to be), crossed the river, formed into a single regiment on the west bank and marched to Hillsboro to quell the activity of a band of "Regulators" who were instigating riots and upsetting the people – early rumblings of revolution.

General Sherman and a portion of his Union Army were encamped here, the final stop on his "march to the sea", when General Lee surrendered the Confederate army at Appomattox in 1865, ending the Civil War. On receiving the news by a horseback courier they celebrated big time up and down the few streets on the east bank of the Neuse.

And the town was in the running for capitol of the state of NC but Raleigh won by a narrow margin. And, in my lifetime, notorious moonshine production and KKK activity have played a role in the undercurrent power structure of the county. Thankfully that era passed a long time ago.

The welfare of the area was deeply rooted in the great number of fertile farms, large and small, where most of the people lived. But the town grew slowly. North Carolina had more farms than any other state in the country in 1940. There were 11,000 mules on Johnston

1

James E. Munden, Sr.

County farms alone at that time, but tractors were beginning to move in.

The Family Farm

My grandparents on my father's side of the family, Isaac and Ophelia Munden, had owned their 111-acre farm since the 1890's and my father, Otho, and mother, Ila, had recently had our house built (around 1923) on a prime spot two hundred yards away from Grandpa's house across a field. The land was of good quality and grew nice crops of tobacco, the money crop and corn for mules that were used for all cultivation of fields as well as pulling wagons for hauling everything that needed to be transported, or for riding around the area. There were peach and apple orchards as well as a forest of plum trees. Gardens flourished with a variety of vegetables, and flowers were growing all over the place, thanks to Grandmammy. It was a peaceful environment in which to live. We couldn't eat all the Irish Gray watermelons Grandpa's patch produced, and his cider mill could be heard whining a half-mile away as we ground apples to pulp when they ripened in the fall. The juice was pressed out and we sipped sweet cider...so good. None of it was wasted as he stored it in large earthenware jugs with corncob corks. I'll bet that was good, too, after ageing a few weeks.

Grandpa and Grandmammy's dwelling house was spacious enough with an inviting front porch with rocking chairs for resting and visiting; and a side porch along the middle bedroom and kitchen - a quiet place to sit after supper or even at night in warm weather. It was quiet except for the crickets and hoot owls - no traffic noise. There was shade from the huge, very old oak tree that towered to the sky, a mulberry tree out by the woodpile, and china-berry trees along the edge of the sandy yard which was kept clear of debris by sweeping with a brush broom. It looked nice after a Saturday sweeping.

There were two ancient log structures, one had been the dwelling house earlier in the 1800's, my father was born in it in 1896, and, facing it 60 feet away, was the old corn crib still in regular use as a utility and storage building. Stables and a fenced-in mule lot extended from the side under more large oak trees. A large shelter housed plows, rakes, hoes and a host of other farm implements. There were two tobacco (curing) barns at the edge of a forest nearby, built of logs, which became very busy during "barning" time in the summer. Heating and curing were done with 4-foot slabs of wood inserted from the outside into a brick furnace that ran through the center of each barn connected to a metal flue system that distributed the heat.

Water was drawn from a scary 5-foot square hole in the ground, 25 feet deep, with a wooden curb four feet high around the top. A wheel and chain mechanism above the well let the bucket down and a full one could be pulled up quickly. All the water used for the animals, washing clothes and household needs came from this well and it was cool and refreshing. A metal dipper for having a drink hung on a nail.

So, the view from the front porch steps was - the well, thirty feet straight ahead, the old log dwelling thirty-five feet to the left and the corn crib twenty-five feet to the right. This 30 x 60 foot rectangle of space shaded by the oak tree at the corner of the log house, was a major playground for all the children, including our cousins, when they came to visit on a Sunday afternoon.

Straight beyond the well and the big oak, across a wagon and car path, was the woodpile which was well stocked with "stove wood", 14 inch blocks of pine wood split up into uniform pieces for the kitchen stove, and, in the fall, a large pile of tree trunks and limbs which would be cut up and split by axe and crosscut saw to fuel the fire in the fireplace. The large black wash pot sat at the edge of the woodpile. Kerosene lamps were the only source of light inside the house at night and kerosene lanterns and flashlights were used outside.

My wife, Jane, grew up in Atlanta in the '20's and '30's with modern conveniences and it is not easy for her to understand that our life style in the early days on the farm was very similar to that of the pioneers 200 years earlier - except we didn't use candles or cook in big pots hanging over the fire in the fire places. But my mother and grandmother did heat irons on the hearth close to the open fire, for ironing clothes, wet a finger and tapped the iron to see if it sizzled - hot enough to iron. Betsy Ross probably ironed the first American flag she made in much the same manner. Clothes were soaked in big black wash pots, heated to boiling by the wood fire underneath, then scrubbed on washboards with Octagon soap in wooden tubs. Long clothes lines, filled with the week's wash, were a normal scene.

Our Dwelling Place

The layout of our new house was much the same as Grandpa and Grandmammy's house except we didn't have the large trees. On the side porch near the kitchen we had a water pump and a metal sink, which was much used for everything that needed washing - vegetables, dirty hands, etc. There was a well nearby, a chinaberry tree and, in the front yard, two cape jasmine bushes beyond the front porch. The yard around the house was sandy and a nice place for us kids to play.

The border of our neighbor's (Breedlove) 109-acre farm was a wire fence in a line of trees in front of our house that extended a quarter mile past Grandpa's house and barns. A two-rutted path ran from their farm through a gap in the fence at the corner of our yard, turned right, following the fence line to Grandpa's house and beyond through the woods to the next farm a half mile away. In the other direction the two ruts bisected the open fields of the Breedlove farm for ¾ of a mile out to their dwelling on the main road, which is now highway 210 from Smithfield west to Angier. It was an active thoroughfare through the countryside but, being unpaved, was either dusty or muddy.

So, in 1924 our family of three and the grandparents were isolated from the main stream of community activity. Only occasionally did a Model-T car or truck come our way down the path. My grandparents never did own an automobile. He used his mule, Maude, and a wagon for a rare trip as far away as Smithfield if he needed to haul something to or from the farm. His quaint buggy was parked under a barn shelter along with a "log cart" which had been used for cutting and "snaking" (dragging) logs out of the forest "low grounds" in times past.

Walking was another much used method of moving from place to place. Since farm work involved constant muscular activity and body motion, just walking seemed easy. Distance didn't matter. My grandmother walked 1½ miles to her church on special occasions. Grandpa roamed all over the woods and streams of the area, hunting and fishing.

Dad and Mom - Otho and Ila

Those of the family who were content with the confinement of a back-woods life style, although quiet and comfortable, did not include my mother, Ila.

She had been born on her family's (Walter and Eleanor Woodall) farm several miles away from the Munden farm - near Four Oaks, in 1899 and had the misfortune of losing her mother in the typhoid epidemic of 1901 when she was only two years old. Her father married a second time and she and her brother, Elijah, being unhappy, left home and moved into their grandmother's home nearby. She spoke lovingly of their relationship and the many practical things she learned at the kind hand of her grandmother - cooking, sewing, gardening, canning and a hundred other homestead related activities. And through the years granddaughter was an eager student who had the drive and desire to learn and the energy to produce. They lived at a crossroads in an active community of plush farms with the schoolhouse down the road. She and Elijah spent much time together working and playing.

Drive and desire were two wheels spinning in the sand on the slow paced, out-of-the-way farm of my father's parents. The atmosphere was calm and work constant from one day to the next, with no goal in sight except to make it through the year, then plant a new crop next spring. So, I am sure my mother felt shackled and upset with the prospect of raising a family in a lonely circumstance. No wonder I saw tears in her eyes when she was alone, washing dishes after a meal. She was out of bed before dawn gathering vegetables from the garden and preparing the day's food before going to other pressing work of the day. Of course my father was up also, already involved with the day's labor. There was little idle time around the farm in spring, summer and fall - winter was easier.

My father was an easy going and likeable gentleman, at ease with the livelihood he had experienced on the farm since birth. He was a veteran of WW I, having been a signalman in the Navy on a troop transport ship. He also was a fiddle player of respectable ability and played with other musicians at square dances, "school closings", fiddlers' conventions and various other community functions. One of my early memories was of musical instruments in the house and a friend or two coming over and playing music by the fireplace. My mother played guitar with the family but didn't play away from home in the early days. There were also baseball gloves, catchers' mitts, bats and balls in the back room, as he was the equipment manager of a local sandlot baseball team. So, my father with a Model-T sedan wasn't isolated - and I am sure my mother went with him when she could. But she nearly always stayed at home with us kids.

The Children - Carlton, Edwin, Julia and Braxton

She said I was a contented baby with lots of dark hair (born August 7, 1924) - no trouble at all. But this wasn't true of my older brother, Carlton, age 2, who, I understand was somewhat troublesome. I didn't remember this, of course, nor do I remember when my redheaded sister, Julia, was born in 1925, who they said was a little feisty and strong-willed befitting the color of her hair. But I do remember when Braxton was born in 1928, and he was a real pill from the beginning - spoiled, since he was the youngest. Fortunately they all outgrew their early childhood attitudes and became really nice kids as they grew up. (Julie and Tom, put that phone back on the hook!)

And I don't remember the day in May, 1926, tobacco-transplanting time, that near-tragedy beset the family when I was playing in the sand bed in the yard at our house. Two mules were pulling a heavy transplanting machine in from the field nearby to refill the water barrel. Grandpa was in the driver's seat on approaching the well when it rolled forward a bit down an incline, bumping the leg of the younger mule, spooking her. She jumped, scaring the other one. They ran in a half-circle around the well, throwing Grandpa to the ground, then headed straight for my sand bed at a gallop. My mother was standing on the porch thirty feet away, horrified, as a mule's hoof kicked me to the ground on my back and the 6-inch wide metal wheel of the transplanter ran straight across my midsection. The runaway mules ran down the road all the way to Grandpa's house before they stopped.

"Limp as a dishrag and turning blue" was the description my mother gave after picking me up and going into the house. My father set out on the long trip to Smithfield to bring a doctor. When he arrived an hour or two later he found me badly bruised, but still breathing. He determined that there were no broken bones or head injuries, and said it was fortunate that I had been in a prone position when the heavy wheel passed over me in the soft sand.

Around The House

By late 1926 my memory began recording some of what I was seeing and hearing. We all slept in one room, a double bed for us three children and one for Mom and Dad. This middle room was next to the kitchen and was where we lived most of the time. In winter a nice fire in the fireplace and another in the cooking stove in the kitchen kept this area comfortable and cozy. We had quilts galore when it was cold. A kerosene lamp or two on the mantle gave off good light, but one was kept burning with low flame when we all went to bed - which was rather early in the evening. Washbasins, soap and washcloths were used for cleaning hands and taking baths. There was warm water in the reservoir next to the firebox on the kitchen stove. An outdoor privy in the trees beyond the yard in back was used during the day and chamber pots were kept inside at night.

These were normal living conditions for homesteads with no running water and no electricity and everybody was quite comfortable and at ease with his lifestyle.

As we children grew a little older, we played with each other and with whatever was at hand to entertain ourselves. I remember rocking violently in my mother's favorite wooden rocking chair. One day it turned over backwards and threw me across the room. But my favorite sport was revving up her Singer sewing machine by sitting on the floor and working the foot pedal with my hands. It would fly - so did the thread. (She thumped me on the head with a hard knuckle when she found it tangled up.) We had a few toy cars, made whirlie-gigs, using large buttons and string, and rolled old automobile tires around the yard as fast as we could run. Julia had a doll or two but preferred the running and jumping activity.

But we were probably bored - not going anywhere, except to Grandpa's, or seeing anybody, except the family, and this bothered our mother in particular.

We had plenty of loving care and attention in every way she could provide. And we were around the table at meal times. There were children's books - she wanted us to learn to read as soon as possible. So, she rocked us on her lap and taught us the ABC's. Her schooling, although adequate for general purposes, was not as complete as she had wished because she had had to go to work and make a living for herself, in her teens. Dad had a good education, too, and at one time had attended a business school in Richmond, VA. He subscribed to a daily newspaper, which he read with interest. He mentioned baseball players occasionally like Mel Ott, Babe Ruth or Jimmy Foxx. Both our parents aimed at getting us children educated to a higher level than they had reached.

In 1928 Braxton was born. Carlton (Tom) was six years old and already helping with minor work around the farm, and was nearing school age. Occasionally someone would ride or walk up to our house and an acquaintance would chat with Mom or Dad for a while. But the ones we began to see most often were our cousins, Aunt Eva and Ernest Laughter's family, on Sunday afternoons. Uncle Ernest liked fishing and hunting, so, the men talked, and Aunt Eva, Dad's sister, and the ladies visited on the front porch while the three of us kids chased around the yard playing games with Eula, Lizzie, Grace and Helen in the shade of the big oak tree. Their two brothers, Marvin and James, were older and had other interests, although we came to know them well, too, in later years. But our childhood bond still brings all the remaining ones together for a special dinner the evenings before our family reunions - now 70 years later.

Around The Neighborhood

Grandmammy's house was becoming a second home for Carlton, Julia and me, and we often ran down there, with permission, of course, when the opportunity arose.

Grandmammy loved having us with her whatever she was doing summer or winter - walking across the woods to cousin Ada's farm on the main road, taking some of Grandpa's cane fishing poles down to Middle Creek fishing, or roaming around the edges of the fields picking blackberries. One spring day we even tried to make a kite of newspaper and broom straw and ran ourselves silly trying to make it fly. But I am sure she enjoyed watching us experiment.

Julia and I are only 14 months apart in age and we teamed up well gallivanting all over the place. One day on a stroll over to cousin Ada's house, misfortune befell her. On the way home we had run ahead of Grandmammy in the cow pasture and climbed the wooden gate to jump over the fence. When we leaped to the ground on the other side a loose board gave way, causing Julia to crash at a bad angle. She got up grasping her left arm and began crying. Grandmammy was very much concerned as we crossed the stretch of woods back home. A doctor was summoned and she was taken for treatment. She had a broken bone in her left elbow and, unfortunately, received a poor re-setting job, resulting in a shorter left arm that wouldn't fully extend. (She said in later years that the shorter arm on the left side gave her better control of her golf swing!)

The wide variety of activities on the farm consumed most of the time of the adults. Early rising, feeding the mules and chickens, early breakfast and off to work - was the routine of the day, Monday to Friday. A heavy meal at noon and a short time of rest were relished as the workload created big appetites. Saturday was slower with maybe a trip to the neighborhood store or to Smithfield to buy the few food items not produced on the farm - flour for biscuits, sugar and lard for cooking.

It was on one of these runs in Dad's Model-T with the top folded down that I recall my first ride through the Breedlove farm, out to the main road and on to Smithfield. The genie was out of the bottle - I have loved traveling ever since.

Sunday was a "no work" day with a complete let-down of activity except feeding the animals. There was a lot of sitting and rocking, nodding or visiting. It was a time for rest.

A New Horizon

School days were about to begin for Carlton. In the late twenties there were the major city schools, (Smithfield was one of the best), and numerous "one room" schoolhouses in localities all over the county. Oak Grove school was the one nearest us, three miles away. The State of NC had been working on a plan to consolidate these rural units with the graded schools in the towns using a network of bus routes. This plan was completed and put into operation in 1930, my first year in school. But Carlton began his education in the late '20's at the one-room Oak Grove school. His children and grandchildren still laugh at his tales of having to walk for miles through snow and ice to get to school - but some of it was factual. He walked ¾ mile through the woods and meadows to the main road at cousin Ada's house, then either walked or rode with Sally Wright, the teacher, 2 more miles to the schoolhouse.

In the fall of 1930 we both walked out to the main road and there we boarded a newly painted orange colored Model-A school bus and rode 4 ½ miles to the spacious brick buildings of Smithfield school. There were five other buses there - school consolidation was underway.

I entered the first grade and Carlton was placed in the second at first but was soon advanced to the third when they found he was learned enough to be in a higher grade.

By this time Carlton was already learning to play violin. Mother had ordered a junior-sized fiddle from Sears-Roebuck catalog when he was six and he had taken to it immediately. Daddy's playing with his talented friends made him a good home-teacher. Music was to become an enjoyable family activity in the coming years as I learned to strum chords on a mandolin and mother played guitar chords with a healthy stroke. Carlton played first violin and Dad played second (alto). They both played guitar, also. (More about music later).

Depression

This year of 1930 was a pivotal one for our family of 6. Braxton was 2 years old, Carlton and I were in school and the great depression had just begun with the Oct., 1929, economic crash. We were probably less affected than many others who depended on a regular paycheck for their livelihood, and the family had no money invested in the stock market. But our pantries were well stocked with several hundred jars of food, which Mother and Grandmother had so diligently canned, when the summer gardens and fields had been plush with fruits and vegetables. But cash was scarce. Prices on tobacco and cotton had fallen to the floor, so things looked bleak for Mom and Dad that fall. But we kids were too young to understand.

A turn of events was about to change out lives - the Breedlove farm next to ours was going to be sold.

Tragedy and a Blessing From the Past

Lena Breedlove, a hardworking soul, her husband and a son, Gilbert, lived in a nice house on the portion of the farm that bordered the main road. Thurston, with his wife and 3 year-old daughter, Florence, were living in a small house on the farm 300 yards away amidst the tobacco fields. Another brother, Donald, and his wife, Dixie, lived nearby.

As I understand it, Mr. Breedlove, the father, a kindly gentleman, and Lena had reared some problematic sons. Gilbert appeared to be laggard and Thurston was a champion worker, but extremely hotheaded. He felt Mr. Breedlove was spending too much time with granddaughter, Florence, riding around in the car - and was really getting worked up about it. He also told him not to take his little girl to Dixie's house anymore. He had a special dislike for Dixie for some personal reason.

One summer day in 1929 Thurston was working in a nearby field when he saw Mr. Breedlove in the passenger seat with Florence on his lap and an unknown driver heading down the little road through the farm. He watched as it stopped at Dixie's house.

Thurston ran home and got his shotgun. Later, when the car came back up the path, he intercepted it and shot Mr. Breedlove through the neck at close range. He died instantly with Florence sitting on his lap. Intentional? …or a scare tactic gone bad?

Thurston went home, cranked up his old Model-T Ford and started driving toward Smithfield. He was chugging down the highway near Wilson thirty miles away when the police caught him. (He was convicted of murder and spent 30 years in jail. Florence grew up and was a student at Mars Hill College, near Asheville, when Julia was there in the mid '40's. Mr. Breedlove's tombstone still stands in Pisgah Church cemetery by the road a stone's throw away from the home place.)

Lena Breedlove's life was shattered, I suppose, and the depression came just in time to double the woe. She lost the home and farm, but she was a survivor and probably made a home for Florence to adulthood and college.

The Breedlove farm was a choice piece of land with a quarter-mile frontage on the busy highway 210 to be. The dwelling house sat in the short side of a curve with the front porch facing the road. On the other side of the road was the nice white sanctuary of Pisgah Baptist Church amid a grove of large oak trees - a peaceful setting.

The price of this desirable spread of land, barns and dwellings had plummeted 90% in value to an unbelievable $2,650.00. Economic poverty had slammed the country as thousands of businesses were lost, millions of mortgages on homes were foreclosed and fewer automobiles, but more walkers, mules and wagons used the roads. Bread lines grew as many with no money or food strived to live. Life had become a nightmare for many.

It was in this dire setting that mother's brother, Elijah, came one day to tell her that she, Ila, he, Elijah and another brother, John, were to share the proceeds from the sale of timber from a tract of land their long-deceased mother had co-owned 30 years earlier.

She had freed her daughter from isolation. You can guess where the money was going to go. This $400 fortune became the down payment on the Breedlove farm - just across the fence from Grandmammy and Grandpa's farm.

I am sure it was a sad day for Grandmammy, seeing her play pals pack up and go away. The ¾ mile might as well have been 10 miles. The daily contact was broken and she and Grandpa were left alone - the empty house to remind them. We would miss their gentle presence.

But our family took to the new house by the side of the road with fervor. The school bus stopped at our front door and Pisgah Church was about to get some new members. It was March, 1931.

The Spring of '31

Planting season was at hand, so land had to be cleared, plowed and fertilized in a hurry. Help was needed but cash for hiring was just about non-existent. It was near this time that Clenzy Hodges, a middle-aged black man, came by and asked for work of any kind. He was glad to get the 40 cents a day Dad was, at times, hard pressed to pay him, and to have a place to call home in our little tenant house by the road. Prices from the 1930 crops had been so low there was little money left, and according to Mother, some of our morning meals were skimpier than she wanted to remember. But Clenzy and Dad worked side by side for months that first year. Mother was busy as a bee, too, preparing the huge garden the Breedloves had tended, building a flock of chickens - anything to help get our new farm to producing whatever could be turned into money - eggs, chickens, and vegetables. Food could be produced in abundance, depression or no depression, and crops could bring in cash, even at a paltry price, but clothing, food, mules, cows and cars could be bought at the same paltry price - so this farm investment could be made to work.

Carlton and I boarded the school bus every day - education was a must.

Mother started going to church across the road every Sunday and shortly had us kids thrown headlong into the graded Sunday School of the Missionary Baptist Church... Dad soon began attending and later was baptized, becoming an active member and later a deacon and Sunday School Superintendent.

Our New Surroundings

Our new house was white like the church. It had a large kitchen, three bedrooms and a living room, all with fireplaces. A forty-foot porch on the front faced the road 100 feet away. Two large chinaberry trees shaded both ends of the porch. This was the resting place on workdays on the noon break. A symmetrically shaped oak tree of monstrous proportions stood across from the kitchen 75 feet away in the side yard. Our 20-foot-deep tiled well curb stood beside the tree. The water was cool and plentiful. Churchgoers walked across the road on Sunday mornings to enjoy the shade and get a drink.

Beyond the big tree were the garden fence, mule lot and stables, feed barn, a hayloft and shelter for farm implements. Two tobacco-curing barns were in the rear at the edge of the fields.

The sandy yard was kept clear of weeds and was swept clean of debris, mostly by us children, on Saturdays when we were resting.

Dad parked his Model-T car under an out-building shelter, near the big oak. Sometimes it wouldn't start up. He had an unusual way of prodding the motor into action. Getting the right rear wheel suspended off the ground relieved the compression in the engine making the crank turn easier and faster. So he backed himself up to the wheel, grasped the wooden spokes and lifted the rear quarter of the car off the ground as I placed a block of wood under the axle. The airborne wheel spun and jerked as he turned the crank. When the engine fired up, the wheel flew. It spun while the engine warmed up, then we pushed it off the block. He could have used his car jack but this was quicker.

The lighting system in the house was unique. Each room had a central light fixture fueled by carbide gas piped into the house from an outside tank. But bright lamps were still used for meticulous work like sewing or reading.

There was no running water or electricity, so cooking and heating were done with wood as before. The three older children slept in a separate bedroom across the hallway. It was unheated in cold weather so we used many quilts. The living room was next to the front porch and we built a fire if company was coming.

We had a nice looking homestead in the long curve. Along the road 500 feet on the west side toward Angier was a tobacco field and a 3-room tenant house, Clenzy's house. On the east side 900 feet toward Smithfield were the feed barn, an apple orchard and an open field at the end of which was a "sand pit" next to cousin Ada's farm. This pit would become an immediate source of a few dollars in cash, as building contractors liked the high grade of sand for concrete and mortar mixing. Their men came and loaded it with hand shovels onto flatbed trucks. They got a bargain at $1.50 a cubic yard.

First Fruits

By summertime gardens were ripening and crops of tobacco and corn looking good. The jars in the food pantry were mostly empty and ready for a new season of canning. Six and seven year old kids could do this as Julia and I found out when mother put us to work mercilessly - picking and shelling beans and peas, peeling peaches or snapping beans for long hours. Carlton was probably working in the fields with Dad and Clenzy.

Tobacco barning time came in July and August and kids could do this, too. Dad hired some extra help, as around 15 "hands" were needed to fill a barn with green leaves strung on 3-foot tobacco sticks. At the end of a hard day's work he paid everybody their wages from a bag of coins. Children my age made 7 ½ cents an hour, adults doing the same job, 10 cents, stringers 12 ½ cents, and the toughest job of all, the men gathering the leaves in the field, 15 cents per hour.

Barning tobacco was fun as it brought out the personalities of the women and children, black or white, in close proximity with each other, doing the mindless job of stringing tobacco on a stick. They told jokes, funny stories and broke out in guffaws. The men in the field always had a funny guy, but one or two worked all day and never said a word.

The tobacco was brought to the barn on a sled pulled by a mule between the rows. Mag was our main mule and was as docile as a kitten. She was ready to go early and, at noon, when she was unbridled, drank a bucket of water and took a hefty wallow in the sand. She was mighty strong.

At the end of the barning day the men loaded the tiers in the barn with about 700 sticks of green tobacco, ready for curing. It took 5 days of firing the furnace, slowly advancing from 100 degrees to 170 to dry the leaves and stems. This process was repeated once a week for six weeks until the stalks were stripped of leaves. Each of the two barns had to be cooled and emptied of the cured tobacco each week before refilling the barn. The only problem was that the one to be filled that day had to be emptied early the same morning beginning around 2:00 a.m. This was the beginning of a long day's work - not to mention that the five days of curing required around-the-clock attention to keep the fire going.

But one of the most heinous jobs to be done was stripping the leaves off the tall corn stalks to bring in a supply of fodder for the mules. The stripper reached with both hands to the top, 7 or 8 feet, pulled the leaves off all the way to the bottom. After 3 or 4 stalks he had accumulated two handfuls. He put these together, tied a knot around the top with one of the leaves, snapped a bare stalk off above the ear of corn and jammed the little bundle on top to dry out. A few days later, on a moonlit night after supper, after some dew had moistened the dry bundles, we hitched Mag to a tobacco sled and went back to work. Four of these small bundles were tied with another leaf or two into a larger one and thrown into a gathering row where they were collected. This was excellent food for the mules for months to come, and it was a rowdy time for the kids hauling the loads to the barn under the stars - sort of like a hayride.

Fodder pulling was such a backbreaking job that some strong and tall men were hired for 2 or 3 days to do the work. Mother prepared a lot of food for their noon meal which was included in the day's pay. Most of these were black men accustomed to the work. They were congenial and ate heartily. We ate early so they could use our table in the kitchen for their meal. The hourly wage in 1931, '32 and '33 was 15 cents.

Back to School

It was late summer and time for school to start up again, and we kids were not too unhappy about that. Entering the first grade, Julia boarded the bus with Carlton and me. We had had a busy summer vacation at our new home preserving food and barning tobacco. This routine would repeat itself in the years to come.

But we weren't finished with the tobacco. It had to be taken off the sticks, graded and prepared for the auction market in Smithfield. This work was done inside the pack barn by Dad, and Mother, when she wasn't busy in the house. Grandmammy walked up from their farm and assisted occasionally. When we came home from school, we joined in, too - sometimes into the evenings. This created some cash flow - to pay the mortgage and buy some school clothes.

Our school bus made two runs in the a.m. and in the p.m. We arrived twenty minutes before the bell rang and waited for the second load in the afternoon, so we had a little playtime on the schoolyard. I soon took to marbles. I suppose this was my first gambling venture and I didn't even give it a thought. Two or three of us boys would draw a five foot circle on the bare ground and each throw in a couple of marbles which were clumped into a pack in the middle of the ring. The first shooter placed his knuckles on the line and thumped a larger marble toward the pack. If he missed, the next one tried. When a marble was knocked outside the ring, it was his to keep, and if his shooter was still inside he could shoot again from that position. It was amazing the skill some of these kids developed. Some could break the pack with the first shot and then clear the ring one at a time. I was about average at this endeavor and stayed away from the sharks.

The school building for elementary grades and another for high school occupied almost a city block with a huge playground adjacent. They were large two-story brick structures with basements. Classrooms were outfitted with about 30 bolted-down desks in neat rows (desks had holes in the upper right corner to hold ink bottles in days past when dip pens had been used). The desks varied in size from grade to grade. Steam heat was effective and quiet, and tall windows could be opened wide for fresh air in warm weather. Two incinerators near the buildings burned all the paper trash rounded up by the janitor after school. A large lunchroom in the basement had a good variety of food. A huge Danish bun cost five cents. We rarely bought anything in there as we took something from home in our tin lunch boxes - usually crackers and peanut butter or a sausage biscuit. Many of the kids who lived in town walked home for lunch.

Autumn on the Countryside

There was still work to be done around the farm in the fall. The thousands of dried ears of corn had to be gathered from the fields, potatoes had to be plowed up, yams and Irish, a turnip patch cleared and planted and collard sprouts transplanted. The supply of wood for the fireplaces had to be cut and hauled in. So there was still plenty of work for Clenzy outside.

Frost would ruin potatoes, so they had to be protected against the cold weather. A unique and very inexpensive way to do this was to construct a "potato hill" that resembled a low-slung Indian tepee. A circle of eight-foot poles gathered at the top around a 4-foot high center post, covered with a thick layer of pine straw and then a layer of dirt made an effective shelter for curing and storing them.

We didn't grow cotton in 1931, but many others did. So the fields turned white when the bolls sprang open. They were beautiful - if you weren't going to be one of the pickers. Family members of all ages could do this, but this was such a slow-moving task that professional help was usually brought in from town where people, usually blacks, male and female, were eager to get the work. This was piecework - 75 cents for picking 100 pounds. A really adept picker could gather 200 pounds in a day. Some used kneepads and shuffled along on their knees, but others worked all day leaning over the plants. They pulled burlap bags, with shoulder straps, behind them, emptied the full ones onto a burlap sheet which was weighed with a tripod and scale.

The sheets were emptied into a two-horse wagon with high rails. Mules pulled the load down the road to Rand's cotton gin a mile toward Smithfield. In October there was a line of wagons and Model-T trucks waiting their turn at the gin. The muffled drumbeat of the steam equipment permeated the air on chilly fall mornings. The wagons came away with a 500-pound bale that would be sold for $40 to $50. A bale per acre was average production.

28

Another intriguing sound that wafted over the countryside on still days was the train whistles of the steam locomotives flying by on the busy Atlantic Coast Line railroad that ran from New York to Florida. It passed through Smithfield and Selma, three miles north. The Seaboard Railway, a major east/west line, crossed the ACL at Selma, making it an important rail junction. Those puffing and hissing engines were awesome. I wondered about the far-a-way places to which they roamed.

The fall of '31 eased into November with a slowdown in the pace of work on the farm. The harvest was in. It had been a good one. Thanksgiving came at an appropriate time for contemplating our good fortune in our new surroundings. We had a one-week break from school so we hiked down the little road through the farm or through the woods to see Grandmammy and Grandpa, bounced rubber balls off the side of the house or barn, and had a nice turkey dinner with cakes and pies. Our mother was a genius at preparing food. We all bowed our heads for Dad's blessing.

Christmas came along and we had another week off from school, so we repeated Thanksgiving. We brought in an eight-foot tree from the woods which mother decorated to her liking with ornaments, tinsel and angel hair. We had a spectacular Christmas tree - without electric lights. There was no lavish array of gift packages surrounding the tree, but we children received something special to play with or wear. And we bought little do-dads for Mom and Dad and wrapped them meticulously with tissue paper and string - no tape. There were also candy, oranges and other goodies we weren't accustomed to having. But not much money was spent as it would be a long time before there would be any more tobacco to sell. And we were all present at Sunday School and the Christmas program at Church on Sunday.

James E. Munden, Sr.

The Dead of Winter

So, 1931 slipped away and '32 ticked in with no fanfare. With the beginning of a new year a few families who had no permanent home, tenant farmers, white and black, began moving along the road at the pace of a mule pulling a wagon, furniture piled high, to a farm up or down the road that would be home for the next year. These weren't desperate people - most were healthy and not unhappy - they just didn't own anything but household belongings and maybe a mule. Many farms had an extra house and mule stable which became a homestead for farm workers who needed a place to live and access to some land to grow food or money crop in exchange for a year's free residency and a financial agreement for labor on the farm. It appeared to be a good arrangement for both parties. Some large families lived on the same farm for years.

But the nation's economy was flat on its back and the ire of unemployed, desperate people was rising to a crescendo of near-revolt against the government, especially President Hoover, who they claimed started it, and wasn't doing anything about it. Banks were failing, businesses were going under at an increasing rate and 12,000,000 workers couldn't find a job to earn even a few coins. (A comparative figure for 2002's population would be 30,000,000). Large industrial cities all had homeless, lean-to cardboard shack residential areas called Hoovervilles to where the penniless drifted. And the bread lines got longer. Occasionally someone would come to our door and ask for something to eat. Mother said she never turned anybody down.

At age eight I was not aware of the hardship that so many people were enduring. The school bus ride was a noisy adventure every day and the games at school and the classes kept my attention and I was happy. We all went to Sunday School and I gave my offering, one penny, then ran out and played after church.

Dad read The News and Observer, a Raleigh newspaper, every day and spoke of what was happening in the world. This was our source of news, as we didn't have a radio. He and Mother went to town occasionally and I recall listening to them talk about their trip. One Saturday Dad had seen a parade of Hoover carts clop down Market Street to the river bridge.

A Hoover cart was a new-fangled contraption built with the axle and two rear wheels of an old discarded automobile. There were plenty of those, so a cheap wooden frame and a seat were constructed above the axle and a pair of shafts attached so a mule could be hitched to it. The rubber tires gave it an easy ride, so these carts became popular with the diminished use of family cars.

So this stream of homemade vehicles paraded down Market Street with music and much ado while the crowds cheered. The winner of the affair was a guitar player who eliminated the mule and hitched himself to his cart, hobbling along and singing "Hoover Stole My Mule".

Political rhetoric was flying. President Hoover was trying desperately to do something to appease the populace. The government had passed a "Bonus Bill" in the early '20's for veterans of WWI to be paid an amount of cash in 1945. There was a clamor for this money to be paid immediately in 1932. . The House of Representatives passed the bill. Veterans numbering 15,000 marched to Washington to pressure the Senate into passing the bill, too, to make it law. They did not pass it. The angry group had to be dispersed by Federal troops.

What We Were Up To In '32

Carlton (alias Tom in later years) had turned 10 on Jan. 21, was in the fourth grade and playing the fiddle with much skill. I, Edwin, (alias Jim), 2nd grade, was admiring my growing collection of beautiful glass marbles, throwing home-made string baseballs back to Carlton who was trying to throw curve balls, and strumming chords on the mandolin in accompaniment with him and Dad. Julia, lst grade, with her beautiful red hair and bangs was - well I don't remember what she was doing, something challenging, I am sure, but she was right in there with Carlton and me racing around the farm. Braxton, only four, was picking up speed but hadn't been put to work yet. Mother was busy thinking of new enterprising ways to enhance our economic position and I think I had been selected as her main helper. And Dad was making plans to take Carlton and me out to some public places, like filling stations, to perform a little music for the Saturday night idlers around the big wood stoves. I recall vividly riding our Model-T to Clifton Beasley's store near the river at Smithfield and playing on a cold winter night to an enthusiastic crowd of about ten gathered around the stove. Everybody was happy and soon Dad pulled his hat off and handed it to me to pass around to see how much they had enjoyed our music. This was a new adventure for me but I did it with a vague smile - and a few coins dropped into the hat. This could pay better than marbles!

I was the newcomer to the trio. Dad, on the guitar and "Otho's boy", who did tricks with his fiddle, were already well known around the community. Carlton's specialty was Pop Goes The Weasel in which he played it on top of his head, behind his back and under his leg. This amused the crowd, but he also played lively square dance tunes up to speed with some of the adult fiddlers. So, I had to pick hard to keep the rhythm. (Dad would lean over and say "Keep up!" if I got a little draggy. More about music later - it was becoming a focal point to our time away from work.)

Some new things, sorely needed, began to appear. Dad acquired another mule, Blackie, younger and feistier than Mag, a Jersey cow that would produce a good supply of milk and a one-horse wagon for moving things around. These would have to be paid for from the new crop we were planting

We would cultivate 20 acres of the best land in tobacco, corn, potatoes and vegetable gardens. Cotton might be added next year. With two mules, spring plowing, harrowing, fertilizing and planting would be made easier. And our tenant house up the road would have a different occupant for the year. Clenzy had found work somewhere else. Mother's half-brother, Eli Woodall, a spry young man of 23, recently married, came to live and work with us. He and his lovely wife, Leola, contributed greatly to lightening the workload and bringing in a good harvest. They soon secured a mortgage on a farm of their own.

But Uncle Eli did our family a monumental service one day. He was drawing a bucket of water from the well under the big oak. I was standing beside the well. Dad was driving in from the road to park under the tree. He was approaching slowly when toddler Braxton came running from the rear and tried to grasp the running board on the driver's side to climb aboard. Dad didn't know he was there. Braxton's hands slipped and he spun under the car in the path of the rear wheel. In a split second Eli yelled, "Stop!" Dad was looking our way, so he reacted quickly and jammed the brakes.... Just in time.... Braxton was flat on his back with his legs spread - one on each side of the wheel. It was inches from rolling onto his groin and stomach.

Grandmammy and Grandpa were grinding away with the annual routine of clearing their fields of dead tobacco stalks, hitching ageing Maude to the turn plow and making ready to plant again. Grandpa, 66 years old, was not aware of the meaning of retirement, so he kept going. They arose at sunup every day - he went to feed Maude and the chickens and she built the fire in the woodstove and cooked biscuits, eggs and pork - and perked coffee. They didn't raise pigs, so breakfast meat was bought along with Nucoa margarine and syrup from the store. Their life was simply a subdued movement from one day to the next. Grandpa walked bent over slightly and a "catch" in his back caused a grimace of pain on his face now and then. I don't know if they owned their land or still had a mortgage obligation. But they appeared to keep their heads above water very well in the tough times.

I am sure their minds were churning with loftier thoughts than farming required. She had written a poetic tribute to her afflicted sister who had lived with them and passed away a few years earlier. It was published in the Smithfield Herald along with the obituary. She kept a diary for years, pencilled in the margins of the Farmers' Almanacs. Her father, a Civil War veteran, had been a music teacher and owned a country store near town. Grandpa had five brothers, three of whom had farms in the area, the others, a career army master sergeant and a mortician. He had experimented with perpetual motion - building a machine with weights, wheels and pulleys. I remember playing with it in their back room. He must have had a bent toward mechanical engineering to be pondering Newtonian problems of physics He read magazines a lot. So there were many thoughts moving through his head while he was plowing corn.

But the two of them were survivors. We kids spent the night with them along with some of our cousins. Grandmammy pulled the big featherbed down onto the floor and we piled on. A few times Carlton and I played the fiddle and mandolin for them. The depression didn't affect them so much, I don't think. They were solid as a rock.

The farmland in the county was cultivated to the maximum in 1932, so, most open fields had tobacco, cotton, corn, soybeans or hay growing on them. The summer countryside grew into a patchwork of green fields that turned golden in the fall. Nearly all the open land was producing something of value. We were fortunate to be living in such a garden spot. (In 2002 most of the small farms have long been absorbed into mass mechanized operations, much land is untended - grown over with pine trees and bushes - buildings left to deteriorate. The farm land in general looks scrubby compared to 1932 when more people lived on their own land and were concerned about how it looked.)

The prosperous appearance belied the fact that the nation was destitute with economic stress, with its future direction swinging in the balance. But this was an election year. And I believe that the steadying voice and message of Franklin Roosevelt was the ray of hope for millions of scared people that turned the tide of the depression. This better outlook grew into a frenzy of anticipation by election time in November and Herbert Hoover was voted out of office in an epic landslide defeat. (Roosevelt was inaugurated March 4, 1933, quickly submitted recovery and reform laws which Congress passed and confidence began to rise in the minds of the people.)

Our '32 summer routine didn't vary much from '31. My day began by running out to the barn and giving Mag and Blackie a bundle of fodder and four ears of corn which they chewed off the cob. Carlton milked the cow, Daisy. She gave two gallons a day which we relished. It had to be cooled, so a metal container was filled and lowered down to the cold water in the well. Everyone who drew water from it had to be careful not to upset the cooler, as a milk-spill would contaminate the water. Day-old milk was poured into a churn and, when it became half-full, was churned by hand, mine quite often, producing a pound of butter. The buttermilk was good to drink and to mix with flour to make biscuits. We staked Daisy out in the green grass where she grazed in a 30-foot circle, as we didn't have a fenced-in pasture.

At noontime we needed some ice for our big pitcher of tea. It was only a half-mile to Herman Johnson's store up the road, so one of us kids hiked up there and bought a nickel's worth of ice - a chunk hacked off a big block in the ice box and dropped in the cloth bag we had with us. On rare occasions when we made ice cream it took fifteen cents' worth of ice to harden it in the hand-cranked freezer. You can't buy ice cream as good as Mother made with her rich mixture of eggs, creamy milk and peaches.

The country stores all accepted eggs in trade for merchandise. Grandmammy now and then brought a brown bag of fresh eggs up to our house and I took them to the store to exchange for a few items she needed. The going rate was 12 1/2 cents per dozen. There was always

3 or 4 cents extra for some penny candy for me and maybe some for the others.

The Church was well attended on Sundays. Some families came from each direction on the road - on foot. It didn't cost any money to walk. There was an oak grove full of automobiles - Model-T Fords and Chevrolets of the 1920's variety, mostly - no new ones. There were no mule-drawn conveyances. Kids mostly came barefooted but were scrubbed up and neatly attired. Adults "dressed up" for Church. Most men wore white shirts and ties and the ladies all wore their Sunday finery. This was in sharp contrast to the work-a-day attire in the fields and gardens.

The 10:00 o'clock Sunday School was very well organized and filled with children. This was a family-oriented church with plenty of adult participation. And the very next year these enthusiastic members built a two-story addition to the front of the sanctuary, complete with bell tower, to provide quarters for the growing classes and extra seats for church services. Building materials were cheap in price while hope for the future was plentiful in the depth of the depression. Preacher Rosser and his absolutely tireless wife were a beacon of inspiration for the community. She coaxed many youngsters into Baptist youth programs like BYPU, GA's for girls and RA's for boys.

And the new church bell tolled over the countryside at service time. For a week in mid-summer a "revival" was held. There were five days of heavily attended evening services led by a visiting minister with evangelical speaking ability. A number of people, young and older, "joined" the church and a few weeks later were baptized in our swimming hole where the main road crosses Middle Creek two miles toward Smithfield. On a Sunday afternoon cars were parked for a long distance on the road on both sides of the bridge. Members crowding a slope on the creek bank, sang "Shall We Gather At The River" as the minister and a helper waded belt deep into the running water and planted a marker at the chosen spot. Then the dozen or two candidates formed a line into the water and each in turn folded his hands to his chest as the minister lifted his arm high and prayed "In obedience to the command of our Savior, Jesus Christ, I baptize you, my sister - (or brother) - in the name of the Father, Son and Holy Ghost". With a firm grasp by the minister and assistant he was leaned backwards below the surface and raised back up. There were some coughing and sputtering but most had held their nose. Some weightier members caused a bit more thrashing about in the water until they regained their footing but they were in strong hands.

Back To School Again

Our active summer was about to end and one day the Model-A school bus came to pick us up for school again - grades 5, 3, and 2. Our vacation from all that work was greeted with enthusiasm as we got back to the marble rings and ball games on the playground at school. Julia was into hopscotch, jump rope and I don't know what all. Braxton was 5 and was probably lonesome when we were at school. But he had his puppy-dog, Billy, to run with. Billy got excited when he heard the school bus coming up the road in the afternoon.

The election came along in November - with an improvement in peoples' outlook for next year. The spring and summer had been a good crop season and many were finding a more solid economic footing, making ends meet, and maybe were feeling better about themselves. But money was scarce.

Thanksgiving and Christmas were celebrated and, soon after the new year 1933 began, the January movement of tenant farmers and renters got underway. Uncle Eli and Aunt Leola moved away from us to their own home and an elderly couple, Mrs. Dippy Flowers and her husband, came to live on our farm. They were a congenial couple - Mr. Flowers did farm work but she didn't. She would give me a piece of cake when I passed her house.

I think it was in the cold winter about this time that mother recruited me to help her build a brooder house, complete with a brick furnace, to begin hatching eggs and raising little chickens in large quantities for a hatchery in Smithfield. We mixed mortar and she laid the bricks for this 6-foot long, oval-shaped miniature tobacco barn-type furnace to be fired with wood from the outside. It worked just fine and soon there were hundreds of "biddies" cheeping and eating like mad in the cozy little barn. Feeding them was part of my job, too. A few weeks later when they had gotten to be frying-size, the hatchery bought them back. Somewhere in between mother made some money. We already had a flock of chickens which supplied fried chicken for Sunday meals. And a free-roaming flock of turkeys was on the horizon. Roaming around looking for them would be my job, also. But the turkey business would come later.

Dad acquired a different car. I guess he sold the canvas-top sedan and bought a used "closed-in" Model-T coupe with roll-up glass windows from the late '20's. It was crowded when 3 or 4 of us climbed in, which was seldom as he drove it very little. I helped him build fires in the wood-fired heaters in Sunday School classrooms at church on wintry days. A large coal-fired pot-bellied heater warmed the large sanctuary. When nobody was there Julia and I played "chop-sticks" on the church piano which was used to accompany the enthusiastic hymn singing of the congregation on Sunday. It resonated in the empty sanctuary. The doors were never locked so we went in and out at will.

In early March the political scene changed abruptly with the inauguration of Franklin D. Roosevelt to the presidency. But a sudden problem had developed a few weeks earlier with the upsurge of a banking panic. It spread across the country as fearful depositors began withdrawing their money. They wanted cash. The "runs" put 5,000 banks out of business by inauguration day on March 4. (Inauguration day was changed to Jan. 20 by the next election). Roosevelt immediately closed all the banks in the U.S., a banking holiday, until the Treasury Department could examine every bank's books. The sound ones were allowed to reopen with help from the Treasury Dept., doubtful ones were kept closed until they could be assisted into a firm position. Many banks never opened again. The "time out" had restored confidence and ended the crisis.

So the hope that depression-weary people had garnered after the election was becoming reality as much reform legislation was passed by Congress in the next "Hundred Days". However, I don't recall people being sad and destitute. In all my contacts with people - neighbors, church, school, at work in the fields or at play, I remember a lot of smiling and happy people. Their income was tiny and costs were tiny also - not a bad balance. The destitute ones were those who had no jobs, and the new unemployment laws were attacking this problem. Prohibition ended and an ABC store would open in Smithfield in a year or two.

May of '33 found us school kids coming home to another vacation of farming. We were bigger, stronger and faster than a year ago, so we could do more work. We could also play our musical instruments with more skill. And we even began singing in church occasionally as a family quartet. Daddy sang bass, Mother sang soprano, and I did alto and Carlton, tenor. Dad had already been singing some with a male quartet. And Blake Thomas, the music leader, began encouraging a group of 15 or 20 to work toward singing at Vocal Unions, meetings of various country church choirs who met during summers at different locations. We would do this in a year or two. Julia was in this group along with her good friend, Mary Elizabeth Thomas, Blake's daughter He taught shape-note music at night sessions at church for those interested.

But it was Carlton's fiddle playing that was drawing attention. Mother joined us on guitar, with Dad playing second violin, and me, mandolin. We were asked to play at a few social get-togethers at peoples' homes or other community affairs. These were happy occasions and much fun, amid toe tapping and hand clapping. Our music was instrumental only - and we didn't play for square dances. (Carlton and Dad had played as a violin, guitar duet in a lot of places before I came along).

On one occasion we were sponsored by the Johnston Cotton Co. to play on a Raleigh radio station. The four of us went to WPTF, the premier station in the area, sat in chairs in a circle around the microphone and were presented as The Munden Family Band. We played with vigor for about 30 minutes - with commercial breaks, of course. (I often think about this experience, at age 9, when I listen to Garrison Keillor's live radio broadcast of Prairie Home Companion on Minnesota Public Radio).

So our isolation of the past was transcending to participation in affairs of church and community. Mother was active in Sunday School for the kids in particular, and was good at helping put on little plays and skits. Children were encouraged to stand up and take part. If we had a special friend it was commonplace to invite him or her to our house for lunch and to spend the afternoon, returning to the church for the evening service. And now and then we kids would go with another family. And, of course, we invited the preacher to our house for Sunday fried chicken about once every two years.

With the increase of our mingling, mother wanted some better furniture, so a nice brown mohair living room suite was acquired - plus a piano. It was time for Carlton to begin "taking" music. So, this room was becoming the music room, in summer with the windows open or in winter with a nice fire in the fireplace. And a visiting fiddle, guitar or tenor banjo player came in occasionally. This was a happy room. I loved to lounge on the plush sofa and read the funny papers on Sunday afternoons. And all of us, except Dad, dabbled with the piano. Mother even picked out tunes of some hymns and Julia became adept at playing by ear ahead of music lessons in the future. And we experimented with using piano bass chords in a 1-2 rhythm along with the fiddles and guitar. This steady background beat added an interesting sound to our music.

Smithfield School was having a great influence on our lives. We were fortunate to be enrolled in one of the outstanding school systems in the state. The administration of this school was superb under the leadership of H. B. Marrow, county superintendent, and A. G. Glenn, the Smithfield School principal for many years. The curriculum was basic with a staff of dedicated teachers who took a no-nonsense approach to instilling knowledge into the students. Emphasis was put on English grammar, geography and history, as well as reading, writing, arithmetic and spelling. And discipline was maintained in each classroom; although some cases had to be referred to the principal's office.

The schools were segregated. Whites and blacks were miles apart in education and social association. Busses ran routes around the countryside and picked up black kids and took them to the all-black Johnston County Training School, a two-story brick building across town. I won't judge the quality of this and other schools for blacks because I don't know; but I doubt they were as well equipped as ours.

Out on the farm we worked side by side with blacks, communicated one-on-one and felt at ease, joking and laughing. The chasm between the races was puzzling to me at times as when I took a bucket of water to the workers in the field and the blacks always waited for the whites to drink first. But separation was the law on busses, rest rooms, theaters, the courthouse and all public facilities, and most blacks abided by the rules as though it didn't matter. But I am sure it did.

The flow of money was not improving as the seasons passed. Prices were still at the bottom of the barrel and would be slow in climbing in the foreseeable future. Harvests were good but did little more than make ends meet. But the economy did seem to rev up a bit with the new administration programs gathering steam. So, as 1933 faded away I believe hope was rising for better days.

The Dirt Road Becomes a Highway

I recall 1934 as the year things began happening all around. The State Highway Dept. had been doing some intense surveying of our dusty road and were now driving stakes into the ground along the right-of-way. When they arrived at our farm we soon saw a row of markers slicing across our front yard and leading straight to our hayloft beside the road. The curve was too sharp and they were going to change it - and they did. They sent a crew to move the building, bringing in huge jacks and rollers I was fascinated with the work of steam shovels and caterpillar graders as they cut away 40 feet of our front yard, smoothed and packed the roadbed of the high-banked curve and laid a coat of tar and gravel. I loved the smell of all that hot tar. And the drivers of the dump trucks were pros at spreading the gravel. They set the motor at a slow reverse speed, opened the tailgate slightly, tilted the dumper, then stood outside on the running board of their topless cabs, facing backwards with one hand on the steering wheel, and dropped a uniform flow of gravel on the tar for 40 or 50 yards until the load was exhausted. They had to do this with the trucks going backwards so to run over gravel instead of tar. They jumped back in and scooted away as the next one in line was ready to go.

We still had 60 feet of yard left which was plenty to sweep and keep clean. Dad built a six-foot driveway bridge across the new ditch on the left side of the yard, two feet above the waterline, and it had to be sturdy, as a variety of vehicles of all weights would cross it. In later years Mother built a concrete walking bridge across the ditch directly between our house and the church to replace a weaker wooden one. She knew how to do everything, it seemed, and didn't hesitate to do it.

Model-T Fords had given way to the Models A and B, and now, in 1934, the new Ford V-8 was scorching the roads - around our farm community, at least. This reflected the new upbeat feelings people seemed to be displaying about themselves and their economic situation.

Ernest Wall, our nearest farm neighbor across the road next to the church, was a good example of a Great Depression survivor. His family of five were diligent workers, always with beautiful fields of corn, cotton and tobacco, and now, a brand new '34 Ford. It was the first new car bought by anyone out our way, I think. The driver and front passenger's doors opened from the front, a good idea for easy access, it seemed, until one was opened against the wind.

They also acquired a Philco radio, battery-run, with a 50-foot antenna wire stretching from the eaves of the house to the top of a 20-foot pole at the edge of the yard. There was some static when tuning in far-away stations like Louisville or Nashville. But the Walls had discovered a new horizon and invited some of our family to come on Saturday nights to listen to the Grand Ole Opry. In a year or two I would go to their house to listen to boxing bouts - Braddock/Baer, Joe Louis/Max Schmelling and others.

It was in the spring of 1934 that Uncle Elijah came to our house at 2:00 a.m. Mother said she heard the car drive up to our back door and she had a chilly feeling that someone was bearing bad news. And he was - their father had died suddenly of a brain hemorrhage.

Grandpa Woodall had six children by his second wife, but I don't recall his ever coming to our house for a visit. Mother and Elijah saw him occasionally and had a good relationship with their half-brothers and sisters. But Mother was saddened by his death and wanted all of us to go to the funeral. Since our car was a one-seater, Dad asked Ernest Wall if he would drive some of us to the funeral. He obliged readily.

We drove up the dirt roads 10 miles to the Woodall farm near Four Oaks - Mother's birthplace. Two hundred yards from the house in an open field was the neatly kept cemetery surrounded by a wrought-iron fence. The burial service took place among the tall tombstones of relatives. I am sure she was pained with thoughts of her mother's untimely death, but nostalgic about her grandmother. (In 1971 Mother asked me to go with her to the old cemetery. We walked into the field and found that the new owner had removed the fence and bulldozed the tombstones into a small circle of brush and weeds. Soybeans were growing over most of the graves. She was sad again to see her family names lying in the dirt.)

This was the year of pigs and turkeys coming to live on our farm. This meant more chores at dawn and dusk as I added them to my care list. We owned a strip of land across the road next to the church cemetery and this became the pig pasture. They loved the swampy area down in the trees but came running when I brought food. So I crossed the cemetery twice a day for years. New graves covered with flowers appeared occasionally. They faded a little each day. A few years later the large mound of dirt would suddenly sink about two feet - the pine box and casket had rotted and collapsed. Someone came and leveled the ground.

Our small flock of turkeys roamed freely around the farm and woods but came in at night. They always flew up into trees to roost, a natural instinct - no fox would find them asleep on the ground. A nesting hen would wander off alone and lay eggs in the woods or brush. I had to follow her to the nest so we could save the babies when they hatched. And when a thunderstorm was brewing Dad or Mom would say "Edwin, go find the turkeys." So the turkeys and I came dripping home together a number of times.

But the flock served us well at Thanksgiving and Christmas. They grew large and healthy. People in Smithfield bought most of them. Some were hit by cars as they meandered across the new highway.

One Sunday morning when the minister extended the invitation to join the church, I went forward. I was the only one that day but a number of others had joined or would join during the revival meetings. There was a long line of us leading down into the water of the Middle Creek swimming hole at the baptizing that Sunday afternoon in August of '34. I was ten years old.

Grandmammy's church, Hopewell Freewill Baptist, was a half-mile away across the woods on another road. In the summertime when they were having revival meeting services at night, she walked through the farm to our house and I walked with her to her church, then 1 1/2 miles back home under the stars. I spent the night with her and Grandpa, had a good breakfast together and walked back home the next morning. (A few weeks ago in August, 2002, Carlton, Julia and I, along with cousins Eula, Grace, Helen and James had dinner in Smithfield on Saturday evening before the Munden family reunion the next day. Grace has been a member of Hopewell and a major figure in the church's ministry for years, so she arranged for our family group of 23 to use the Activity Center for a couple of hours after dinner. Julia's family had come from Virginia and Florida, my son from Charlotte and my daughter from Michigan - It was the best visit our family had had in decades. The church brought back many memories. Grandmammy and Grandpa's tombstone marks their graves in a plot beside the building.)

Our string music, as it was called, hadn't let up at all. An article in The Smithfield Herald of 1934 tells about Otho Munden taking his 12 year-old son, Carlton, to a fiddlers' convention. Being too young to enter the competition for prize money, he was asked to play a piece just to entertain the audience. They passed the hat for donations. Carlton's "prize" exceeded that of the first place winner. .

When school started in the fall, there were four Mundens waiting for the Model-A Ford school bus in the broad paved curve in front of Pisgah Church. Braxton was joining the fray. He had been left at home with Mother and Dad for two years, but I am sure he had gotten special attention and some home lessons before beginning school. His dog, Billy, was now left alone. All of us were regular school attenders and apparently doing well as our names began appearing on the "Honor Roll" published in the Smithfield Herald.

1935 And Beyond

By 1935 it seemed that the economy had stabilized to the point that people were making ends meet in their money matters. But market prices for tobacco and cotton were not rising and Dad was still paying farm workers from the bag of coins. Ernest Wall's new Ford had cost only $525, so, by comparison, one could buy a lot of smaller necessities with a handful of quarters and dimes. This level of pricing would continue for years to come. The important thing was that many more people were able to find a job of some sort. (Years later, in 1941, I worked on Saturdays in a grocery store in Smithfield, 8:00 a.m. to 11:00 p.m. for $1.50 — 10 cents an hour. At lunch I paid 10 cents for a hotdog and 5 cents for a Pepsi.)

Dad changed cars this summer, updating to a Model-A Ford sedan. A local artisan built him a sturdy farm trailer for $50 and this became a much-used piece of equipment as we hauled everything from fertilizer to people all over the farm and tobacco to market.

Carlton's pitching arm was getting stronger and we played baseball on the school grounds a few minutes before and after classes and at lunch. The string balls were now covered with black tape. Store-bought balls, bats and gloves were rare. He was the first in the family to take piano lessons and took to reading music readily because of his working knowledge of violin. (Three years later after also studying under a violin teacher, Wilhelmina Utley in Benson, he performed a complicated classical piece in her violin recital)

Our family band played at some community affairs and Carlton, Dad and I began playing occasionally with two brothers, Archie and Wilbur Brown. Wilbur played guitar and Archie, tenor banjo. I don't think 5-string banjo playing was common at that time. Earl Scruggs hadn't come along yet. But Wilbur's guitar, Carlton's lead violin and Dad's 2nd, along with the strumming of the banjo and mandolin, produced a deep rhythmic blend. When a piano bass beat was added it was downright good for toe tapping. Square dancers and cloggers would have liked it, too. On one occasion we played in a variety amateur show before a large audience. A tap dancer won first place. Also, one of the local tobacco warehouses produced a stage show of small circus acts with assorted music in between. The Munden Family Band played their hearts out somewhere amidst the hoopla.

In the fall of 1935 Emmett Johnson, a Ford salesman, drove a new 1936 Ford V-8 out to our farm to show Dad. What a pretty car! We didn't buy it. Our Model-A was doing fine.

Our hikes up to the store to get ice for tea were about to end as mother constructed a 3x5 foot ice box of wood and a metal interior insulated with 6 inches of sawdust. Now we could buy a 100 lb. block from the ice truck that came by each week. This would cool milk, too.

The fish man came up the road on Thursdays and Mother bought 7 pounds of trout or croakers, a heaping meal, which she fried to perfection.

Rawleigh products were sold by a traveling salesman with a chicken coop tied to the front bumper of his Chevrolet sedan and a back-seat store of household items most likely to be needed by his customers. He took chickens in trade for toothpaste, lotions, candy, etc.

Lightning rods had been installed on the house when it was built, and when a thunderstorm was coming up we dug a hole at the base of each rod and poured a bucket of water in it to assure good electrical contact with the ground. (A few years later lightning struck the house and destroyed a radio, but the rod had grounded the bolt, doing negligible damage to the house.)

Church activities now included "Harvest Day" in which members pledged farm-produced items to be sold at auction to raise money to run the church. Summertime picnics were spread on a 50-foot wire-fence table stretched between trees, supported by cross bars and covered with white tablecloths. The sections sagged under the weight of a bounty of food. These farm ladies could cook!

Our choir group of about 20 started singing in "Vocal Unions" with several churches, Sunday afternoons, in the summertime, once a month. Preacher Rosser had passed away and A. C. McCall had accepted the call to Pisgah Church.

Grandmammy and Grandpa acquired a battery radio which opened a new door for them - a major source of entertainment, something that had been lacking in their lives. Grandmammy soon began talking about the interesting things she was hearing on the radio.

The highway traffic was growing heavier and faster. There were no white lines in the middle and speeding cars would blast away on their horns as they entered the long curve. Some didn't slow down for an animal in the road. A teenager of the Hobbs family who lived 2 miles west knew only one speed - wide open - when he came down the road in the family Model-A Ford. And my great uncle Needham Munden drove his ancient Model-T coupe at the lower end of the speed range - a steady 25 m.p.h. The new pavement was a thrill for everybody.

The church acquired two or three surplus school busses and brought in lots of people on Sunday mornings. Adam Whitley used his flatbed farm truck with side railings and cane chairs to bring people to church, also. Some new '36 Chevrolets, Fords and Plymouths began appearing in the grove of trees as peoples' financial positions stabilized.

Franklin Roosevelt won the '36 presidential election in a landslide victory over Alf Landon. His anti-depression programs had worked well. But overseas some troubling events were taking place. Italy had attacked Ethiopia and was now occupying the country. The vicious Spanish Civil War erupted. Germany would take this opportunity to test their newly designed aircraft by giving aid to the side of General Franco - good practice for WWII.

All this was in our daily newspaper, The News and Observer, and I recall reading about it as I entered the seventh grade at school. Teachers encouraged us to stay abreast of current events. On the farm our chicken business had gotten larger as we now had a facility to take care of 300 laying hens. The hatchery not only bought the eggs, but the chickens when we were ready to sell.

My favorite family to occupy our tenant house was Arthur Miller, his wife, Sue, and three teen-agers, two girls and a boy. Arthur was a congenial black man with a hearty snicker of a laugh who wore leather boots laced up to his knees winter and summer, worked diligently and enjoyed a little "embalming fluid", as he called whiskey, on Saturday nights. Sue was overweight and a little cranky - but no trouble. Arthur would say on some occasions "Sue ain't got all her buttons." But he had all of his, as well as his well-mannered children. Pearl, about 16, was a beautiful girl with a big smile and apparently well educated. She talked about wanting to go to Baltimore to get a job. She didn't see much opportunity at home. They lived on our farm for two or three years. Arthur had good common sense and more knowledge than we knew, I suspect. In 1938 when King Edward abdicated the English throne to marry Miss Simpson, Arthur took to calling me "King Edwin". He drove our car and trailer around the farm as needed, and sometimes on Saturdays rode with us to Smithfield. One Christmas we were in town on Saturday and Arthur, a bit tipsy, got picked up by the police for exploding cherry bombs on the sidewalk. Dad went to check on him and they released him to Dad's custody if he would take him home.

Rural electrification finally reached highway 210 in 1938 and they planted a row of power poles past our farm. Some people moved quickly to get their houses wired, and bare light bulbs hung from ceilings with more light than these rooms had ever seen. Others took their time about changing, as they couldn't afford it yet. So, it was a gradual process - not a sudden electric revelation.

Julia and I began our piano lessons about this time. Mrs. Eula Hood Stevens lived on S. 2nd St in Smithfield, which was on our school bus route going home. After school we walked to her house early enough for our lesson and the bus picked us up after making its first run. I had Tuesdays and Fridays. And I wish I had had more innate musical ability than I possessed. Music lessons were work for me, and in three years I progressed far enough to play "Scarf Dance" by Chaminade for my recital piece in 1940. But that was the extent of my musical endeavor - until I joined church choirs in later years. This early experience enabled me to "keep up" with the other musicians and I am grateful for what Mrs. Stevens taught me. Julia and Carlton became much more adept with music, but none of us, including Braxton pursued music beyond a secondary experience. Braxton took some lessons, also, but mostly played by ear. He had learned a Boogie-Woogie tune to perfection, but this was the only tune he knew worth performing. He told of an experience while he was in the army, around 1948, at a party gathering. He sat down at the piano and a small crowd gathered as he rendered "Boogie-Woogie" as long as he could extend it. There was applause and a demand for more. He stood up, looked at his watch and made a fast exit saying "Sorry, I have to go." The family laughed many times in later years when this was mentioned.

Carlton's music was "for real" and he would have done well had he pursued it. He performed solo violin pieces through the years and once on a golf trip in the NC mountains was challenged by an ex-champion clogger in the group to perform a duet on the stage of the tavern where they were having dinner. Carlton (Tom, to them) surprised all the golfers when he borrowed a fiddle from the house musicians and struck up a tune. Jack Runnion, the clogger, still laughs at the applause they received.

Baseball was to be his sport of choice. I recall he read the sports page and followed the great major league teams and players of the 30's - Dizzy Dean, Carl Hubbell, Lou Gehrig, the St. Louis Cardinals, NY Yankees and all the rest. His arm was growing stronger playing with a sandlot team nearby, leading to pitching for the Smithfield High School team in 1939.

My own athletic participation was limited to schoolyard games of baseball and softball. But Julia pursued basketball with fervor and she, too, made the Smithfield Hi team in 1942. Braxton, as I recall, wasn't too much interested in sports. Living five miles away posed a problem for after-school practice sessions. But Carlton and Julia did it - arranging a ride home late in the day.

But we were well positioned to drive the school buses. A 1936 Ford had been added to the fleet of six and in 1938 Carlton became its driver on a six-mile route, mostly on dirt roads. So all of us boarded the bus in our back yard. He graduated the next year so Julia, Braxton and I again boarded the Model-A, still in use on the paved highway. My 16th birthday came in August, 1940, and Principal Glenn drove out to our farm one Sunday afternoon and asked if I would take Carlton's old dirt road route, and I did. I had learned to drive our car around the farm and local area and had just gotten my driver's license that week, so my driving experience was nil. School started a few weeks later and I picked up 70 kids, filling the 4 long, cushioned benches. Some of the smaller ones had to sit on someone's lap or stand up. (I drove this route for 2 years and the passenger load remained constant at 69-72 passengers - overloaded by today's rules.)

Where In The World Did Everybody Go?

By 1940 Highway 210 was getting some new traffic - military convoys. Fort Bragg was 50 miles away but our road intersected another, which led to the army base, making this a good secondary route to and fro. The beginning of WWII in Sept., '39 had banged the warning bell that our country should build up our defenses, beginning at once, and military bases had to be expanded, and a thousand other build-ups of materiel and personnel put in motion - in other words, the Great Depression was over. The early morning traffic on our road had been picking up as carloads of men were driving back and forth to new construction jobs at Fort Bragg. And as the months passed convoys of trucks loaded with soldiers, jeeps and vehicles towing guns roared past. Some of the men whistled at tall red-headed sister, Julia, and she waved back with a big smile.

The radio and newspaper were ablaze with war news from Europe, and it was all bad. Carlton was already draft age and I wasn't very far behind, so we watched with interest. Farm activity was continuing as usual and Mother and Dad were as active as ever. President Roosevelt was elected to an unprecedented 3rd term in 1940. Germany was overrunning France and it was becoming obvious that the USA would be drawn into the spreading firestorm.

England feared for its life as it was the next target for obliteration, and the first air attack came that fall - bombs fell by the thousands on London. The British didn't surrender, but were too weak to launch an attack across the Channel, so, Hitler turned eastward and attacked Russia. Japan joined Germany and Italy in an alliance that posed an awesome threat to the rest of the world. In December, 1941, all our efforts to not become involved in the war came to a sudden halt when Japan destroyed part of our fleet at Pearl Harbor - and I was seventeen.

War was declared against Japan and our country began mobilizing at a furious pace - men were volunteering and being drafted by the millions (16,000,000 by war's end.)

In 1941 Carlton had enrolled in Smithdeal-Massey Business College in Richmond, the first to leave home. After completing the course a year later he enlisted in the US Navy in September, 1942, as Yeoman 3rd class. Shortly afterward, he applied for the navy officer training program, V-12, and was assigned to Carson-Newman College in Tennessee.

Julia continued high school for an extra year in the fall of '42; she and Braxton, age 14, remained at home with Mom and Dad.

And I, Edwin, finished the 12th grade in May, '42, attended Smithdeal-Massey for a few months, then volunteered for service in the US Navy on Dec.14 at age 18.

1942 was as bleak-looking as 1931 had been. Our allies in Europe had been pummeled, Japan was entrenched in Southeast Asia, had fortified scores of Pacific islands and Germany was sinking cargo ships by the hundreds in the Atlantic. Russia was in a death struggle with Germany, having already lost a million or more soldiers.

Who was going to win this war? Millions of our youngsters said they would go and try.

"Do You Swear???"...."I Do.!"

There were seven of us recruits sworn in that Monday morning in Raleigh. By mid-afternoon we had boarded a train for San Diego, all on one ticket, heading west. We pondered over why we would be sent cross-country when our largest naval bases were on the Atlantic side. But, what the heck – we had stepped into a whirlwind – a great adventure – to God knows where – and we might not come back.

Then we decided, oh boy - California!

The first episode of the great adventure was about to happen. Wednesday morning at 7:40 we were making our way through the crowded train station in New Orleans. We stopped near the gate and another fellow and I informed our group-ticket holder that we needed to go to the rest room. When we came back the group had left. We frantically searched the big rest room, food bars, and the surrounding crowd of people, but they had disappeared - apparently boarding the train without us. It was getting near our departure time of eight o'clock so we asked the official at the gate, which was the train for California. He said, "The Southern Pacific, right here". We jumped on and began another search. The train was rolling when the conductor asked for our tickets. We explained our "group ticket" situation and told him we couldn't find our buddies anywhere on the train. He then shocked us when he said, "There was another train, the 'Santa Fe', that left at 8:00 also, en route for San Diego, and they are probably on it."

They were aboard it and we were about to be de-boarded from the Southern Pacific. The conductor was understanding and tried wiring ahead to the other train. They couldn't solve the problem and, later in the day after riding across Louisiana, we were given the choice of buying tickets or getting dropped off at a naval base we were approaching on the border at Orange, TX. We didn't have enough money to buy tickets so we took our chances on dropping in for a surprise visit with the folks at the navy base - after all, we belonged to them now.

When we stepped off the train we saw a Navy chief petty officer among the few people on the dock. So, we marched up to him and said, "We are in the Navy going to California and we got separated from the group with the ticket back in New Orleans and got on the wrong train. The conductor said you would take care of us here." The gruff old chief just had to tell us what he thought of our goof-up. He said sternly, "Fellows, in the Navy you don't miss your train! Remember that." Then he went with us on their shuttle bus a few blocks to the base and took us into the Officer-of-the-day headquarters and presented us to the officer with "These fellows are in the navy and they missed their train." The OD was kind and after getting the details about where we had been inducted and where we were going, made arrangements for us to stay there until they could wire Raleigh and get us a new set of orders.

Orange was a small town in 1942 and the base was small also. It was used for personnel waiting for assignments to ships in the fleet. We were free to leave the base during the day, but were afraid of being incarcerated when we arrived in California as we would be three days AWOL!

Our own tickets arrived on Friday and we departed early Saturday. We rolled into the beautiful San Diego area Monday afternoon and made our way to the check-in gate at the Naval Training Station. At a large office with numerous navy personnel busy as bees, we walked up to the open window-counter and presented our papers. The meticulous yeoman studied them for a minute and then he paused and yelled across the room words that still ring in my ears - "Hey, Joe! Here is the rest of that half-assed bunch that came in from North Carolina last week!"

Our dignity was destroyed and we waited quietly for the next calamity. But it didn't come. Things got better as we were processed and assigned to a company without any mention of AWOL. I searched the area and found some of our separated original group but never did see the ticket holder. They had arrived on Friday and were two companies ahead of us - (160 men per company).

"Forward, March!"

Boot camp, in which we wore leggings, lasted until late March and we didn't leave the base. The acres of barracks and parade grounds were splotched with camouflage paint to make it appear to be meadowlands to any foreign aircraft that might be in the area. The military was nervous about the Japanese submarines sighted offshore, so camouflage was commonplace around military installations and factories. North Island Naval Air Station was across the bay to the east, and San Diego was a major harbor with much activity. Seaplanes took off and landed in the bay. Air raid drills were held regularly and thousands of us ran for the high ridge that extended down the coast to Point Loma, at the entrance from the ocean. There were 30,000 navy personnel quartered here. There seemed to be a fear of a surprise raid on our coastline.

The day began with a bugle call, lights went on at 5:00 a.m. and the company lined up and marched out to the parade ground in the dark where all the other companies were gathering to await their turn to march off to breakfast. There was always brass band music coming over the loudspeaker system. After a break we marched off again to the activity of the day, which could have been jumping off a 20-foot tower with a life jacket and underwater swimming exercises for survival in burning oily waters. We learned how to man oars in a lifeboat, how to shoot .45 cal. pistols and .30 cal. army rifles, how to wear a gas mask tightly without leaks, how to get into a hammock five feet off the deck, (carryover from WW1 as we never used the one we were issued), and took aptitude tests for further specialized training. After three months we began to feel better about ourselves - discarding the leggings and going off the base and downtown to the fun city of San Diego.

The aptitude tests revealed that I might have the ability to read the dots and dashes of Morse code, and I didn't know it then, but they weren't finding enough men to train for this job. So, soon I found myself in a class of 120, wearing earphones and deciphering the beeps of the coded system used worldwide for short wave, long distance communication. Coded messages were transmitted in 5-letter groups, like fgsnx, ahpvb, etc. So, there might be 10 of these groups or 200 in a message. When these were typed into the decoding machine it printed the message in plain language. Mistakes in reception resulted in garbled messages. Accuracy was important.

The goal of the three-month radio school was to train the students to receive 22 of these 5-letter groups per minute - that's 110 letters or about 330 beeps each minute. The coded communications transmitted from Honolulu to the entire Pacific fleet were done at near this speed, so radiomen needed to be proficient in their jobs.

Our class graduated in June, 1943. They gave me a third class petty officer rating for finishing in the upper 50% of the class. It was nice having a red chevron and sparks insignia on my sleeve.

We soon got the news that the Marine Corp wanted some of our new radiomen to carry the "walkie-talkie" radios ashore on their backs - choice targets for enemy snipers - in the upcoming amphibious assaults they were about to make on islands in the South Pacific, recently fortified by the Japanese. Tarawa was just around the corner. They didn't ask for volunteers - they transferred the top half of our group, 60 men, beginning with A and reaching into the M's, to the Marine Corp. The hardy Marines suffered many casualties in the horrific "D-Day" experiences during '43, '44 and Iwo Jima in 1945 - and I almost got in on the ground floor. I don't know how many M's they took, but Martinez from Los Angeles was one of them. "Munden" was close.

A nine-day leave was a nice break from a hectic 6 months, but I couldn't travel to NC in so short a time, so when my friend, Herman Rhoda, of Boling, TX asked me to go home with him, I did. Maybe I should have stayed on Mission Beach in San Diego.

Two smoking locomotives were used to pull the long train over the mountain range east of San Diego, heading for Texas. We were approaching Yuma, AZ in the afternoon and they stopped to take on water. One of the engines malfunctioned, so the evening found everybody off the train wandering around and later sleeping on the grass under the trees as the train was dead. They revived it by the next morning and we chugged off. Arizona, New Mexico and West Texas are hot in the summertime and the load of sweaty passengers was getting grimier and more uncomfortable from border to border. The windows on the old train could be raised, and they were - so soon we were getting air and ashes wafting through the passenger cars. Finally, we reached San Antonio and at a town east of there, near Boling, Mr. Rhoda picked Herman and me up in his Model-A Ford and we drove home. His parents were so happy to see him and they treated me like another son. We drove all over town and saw his friends, then went to a dance on Saturday night. There were dozens of army guys there, but Herman and I were the only navy. One more night and we were on the rails again.

When we were attending radio school our company lined up each morning in formation in front of our barracks. The building across from us housed a company in Quartermaster school who lined up facing us 10 feet away. Each company had a member designated as commander who was positioned in front of his unit. Their leader was Henry Fonda, who was already famed as an actor. We had a close look at that poised and congenial gentleman pacing about between our groups. He was 32 years old and it was said that he wanted to begin military service as an enlisted man. (In his biography on TV recently, he was pictured in his enlisted uniform with Quartermaster rating. He later received a commission and served as an officer on a battleship.)

San Diego was abuzz with activity of all kinds. There were always military airplanes flying about - PBY's, P-38's, Liberator bombers. Sailors and Marines added heavily to the population. Nightclubs, bars, stage shows and dance halls were all busy. Al Donahue and his orchestra played at Pacific Square a number of times. The famous San Diego Zoo was already an attraction in 1943. Mission Beach was a big playground for servicemen and a visit to La Jolla Cove, further north near Tory Pines, was a special treat. The spare time we had was fun but the navy had plans for us, most likely at sea.

"Ship, Ahoy!"

A few days after returning from Texas, orders came to report to Pleasanton, CA, near San Francisco, for further assignment. A radio school classmate named Moore was in the group as we rode the luxury train, The San Joaquin Special, 500 miles north through the plush valley. The base at Pleasanton was a dispersion point for assignment to the fleet, much like Orange, TX, only here I felt like a member of the family instead of a lost stepchild. They marched large groups of us up and down the hills to keep us focused, as there was little to do. Every third day we were free to go into Oakland and San Francisco for 24 hours, from noon to noon, a hitch-hiking trip of 40 miles. So, a few weeks passed and we had fun exploring the big cities. Smithfield, NC didn't have anything to compare with this! Finding a place to sleep was a problem, but fortunately the nice hotels helped the overflow situation by opening their lobbies at midnight to servicemen to sleep on sofas, chairs and carpets. I recall the St. Mark (?) in Oakland as a favorite. The Shore Patrol came in at 5:30 a.m. and woke us up. The doughnut shop across the street did a bang-up business every morning as the jukebox blared. My favorite song was "In The Blue Of Evening" by Frank Sinatra, and I still like it.

July passed and I had my 19th birthday in early August, waiting for the roll of the dice to determine my next destination. It came a few days later when Moore and I were told to pack our seabags, and we were soon on a Navy bus en route to the SF harbor. Both of us were assigned to an anti-submarine escort ship - rigged for minesweeping. It was the USS Token, 220 feet long, 32 feet wide, with a crew of 110 men. It had been built in Chickasaw, AL, spent some time in the Atlantic, then passed through the Panama Canal into the Pacific to San Francisco. They apparently needed two more radiomen before heading for the South Pacific war zone.

It was already dark when we arrived at the dock where the ship was tied up. My impression of the sea-going navy had always been destroyers and cruisers cutting the water at high speed accompanied by fearless battleships crashing the waves. But Moore and I were about to be introduced to the "Donald Duck Navy" - the lesser ships. They told us ours was at the end of the dock - but we couldn't see a ship. As we carried our bags on our shoulders we saw the mast and crow's nest, and, getting closer, the bridge at about eyelevel. The main deck was way down there about 7 feet above the water. My first thought was, "They aren't going to take a little ship like this out into the ocean looking for the enemy, are they?".... Yes, they were.

We crossed the gangplank, were logged in and assigned sleeping quarters in a compartment below the main deck near the diesel engines. After getting some food we were directed to the radio shack where we met the two radiomen onboard. They were glad to see us as their senior operator was being transferred. They were experienced at the job - Al Zaffran, 2nd class petty officer, and Art Zook, 3rd class. Both were from Chicago as I recall. So, when Moore and I learned the ropes we would have adequate manpower for around-the-clock radio coverage.

For two or three days we cruised San Francisco Bay with our sister ship, the Tumult, calibrating instruments. We were obviously going to depart soon, so when I was ashore I wrote a short letter home telling the family they might not hear from me for some time as I was going to sea. And the next day we were restricted to the ship and told we would be sailing the following morning.

The news brought out a variety of reactions from the crewmen amid speculation that we would be gone for a long time, maybe 2-3 years, if we didn't run into trouble - which was entirely possible since we were going to where our navy and the Japanese navy were trying to sink each other. Jocularity and rough horseplay picked up and a few began whacking each other's hair off with scissors. They were getting slaphappy at this change in our outlook. The hair chopping fad spread and by the next morning probably 30-40 of them looked like shorn sheep as we steamed under the Golden Gate Bridge along with the Tumult and 12 loaded freighters we were leading to our New Hebrides Island base in the South Pacific. Our destination was unknown to everybody until the captain opened the sealed orders two days at sea.

The bay had been a little choppy and I had had a queasy feeling in my stomach cruising around for 2 or 3 days. I had been on deep-sea fishing boats without getting seasick so I thought I had a strong stomach. But when we encountered heavy seas off the coast and this 200 ft. vessel began rolling, pitching and throwing up salt spray, my stomach gave up and I became violently sick, with the Golden Gate still in sight. Moore was sick, too. The rest of the crew had no problem with the never-ending motion as they had been on the ocean long enough to adjust. Zaffran and Zook had told us about the trip up the coast to New York and the Cape Hatteras waters being so rough. But, for me, it would take a long time, 2 weeks, and a loss of ten pounds, before I could hold food on my stomach. Moore and I both had a bad experience with seasickness as we had to take our turn with the radio watches, 4 hours on and 8 off, dragging ourselves down to our bunks then back up to the radio shack, plus standing up for one hour at "general quarters", battle stations, at sunrise and sunset each day. These were the most likely times that an enemy submarine would attack the convoy.

Zaffran's battle station was manning the radio, so the other radiomen had assignments elsewhere - mine was loading shells into a 20 millimeter anti-aircraft gun on the starboard mid-deck near the smokestacks. These guns fired six-inch-long projectiles at the rate of 7 per second, in short bursts so as not to melt the barrel. There were asbestos gloves and a metal tube filled with water for cooling the hot ones. There were 3 men on the crew, the strapped-in gunner, a loader and a barrel maintenance man. Circular containers that hooked into the breech mechanism on top of the gun had been pre-loaded with 60 shells each. My job was to dismount the empty one and lift a full one into place as needed - which could be quite often depending on the rate of fire. A full one weighed 50-60 pounds.

The first day at sea had been misery for me, but in spite of my condition, things were buzzing. The convoy had shaped into a 4x3 rectangle, the Tumult was busy on the left side pinging with its sonar in sweeping circles, running ahead and looping back to the rear, and we were doing the same thing on he right side. (On this five-week voyage the freighters logged 5,000 miles and the escort ships, 10,000). Convoy speed was 6 knots. The radio was tuned to Honolulu and the radiomen began compiling the log of hundreds of coded messages transmitted daily to the Pacific fleet. I was on the radio for 4 hours with a bucket by my chair, hooked to the deck so as not to slip and slide. Earlier the boatswain's mate had told me where to get a helmet and lifejacket, but after the watch I had collapsed on my bunk for a rest. I was too sick to eat, so I slept through chowtime. The blast of the "general quarters" buzzer frightened me to my feet (I hadn't undressed - it was a law that you slept with your pants on for quick response, but I still had my shoes on, too). The alarm sounded so urgent. When I arrived at the battle station the two gun crews were dressed in helmets and lifejackets, uncovering, loading and cocking the guns. I am sure I didn't look ready to fight, bareheaded and all, but they showed me how to load the gun, and made no comment.

There was chitchat while we looked out over the ocean for periscopes as darkness fell. Our firepower consisted of a 3-inch gun on the bow and another on the rear upper deck near us, about eight 20-mm guns like ours, two fifty-cal. machine guns and tons and tons of 300 and 500 pound depth bombs to drop on enemy submarines. There was never a spark of light allowed above decks - complete darkness. We were in near darkness when an explosion rocked us like a lightning bolt striking the bridge 40 feet away. The flash lit up the sky. I immediately thought, "Here I am in combat already - without a helmet and life jacket."

There was a short time of scurrying about, yelling and general confusion when the loudspeaker announced that someone had accidentally pulled the trigger on the bow gun. We were relieved that we hadn't found trouble the first day out, but the convoy probably started watching the Token with a skeptical eye.

Sailing, Sailing....

The flotilla trudged on. Each day was becoming like the one before. Sunup showed the same formation - our radar and TBS, (talk between ships) kept them from straying off course. Only the weather changed from day to day. The seas could be smooth with lake-size ripples one day and uneven with mountainous waves and deep valleys the next. It wasn't stormy - the sun was bright and it was getting warmer since we were sailing southward. And my energy level wasn't rising above zero, as I still couldn't hold food on my stomach. The workload stayed constant, the diesel engines droned in my ears when I tried to sleep and the general quarters buzzer was making a deeper impression on my brain than the Morse code. But I was able to type those radio messages without any complaints – the accuracy of decoded messages exposed your ability as a radioman - and was dressed for action with a helmet and life jacket when the alarms sounded.

Then, two weeks and 2,000 miles at sea I found I could retain some Ritz crackers on my stomach and I ate a lot. This was the beginning of physical recovery and a return to life and health. Moore did the same, as everyone had known that we would, so we became part of the jolly crew.

Our sonar men had been actively pinging the deep waters, but so far had not contacted anything other than schools of fish - no "burps" like the hull of a submarine would make. It is a big ocean and odds on our not being detected were good, although our shipping routes were well known to the Japanese navy. I am sure there was a lot of valuable cargo aboard that group of merchant ships.

One day our radar showed an unexpected blip 30-40 miles over the horizon to the north. Our captain, Hudson, whose pet parrot had left his shoulder perch and flown away a few days before, like the dove from Noah's ark, was concerned that someone might be stranded and needing help. (The parrot didn't come back). So, we left our perch and steered on a course that would take us out of sight of the convoy for several hours. This seemed to be a risky diversion as our mission wasn't to identify stray objects in the middle of the ocean - it could have been an enemy submarine charging its batteries. After cruising at full speed for an hour or two we sighted a freighter floating high in the water and apparently not moving. Getting closer, we could see no identifying flags or numbers and got no response from blinker signals. It was dead in the water with no signs of life aboard. It was spooky - a ghost ship, or was it a disguised gunship!? We were relieved to get back into the company of our convoy. And our fuel was running low from running our circular patrol pattern. But we had a gas station right there with us.

A few days later we did have to fill our tanks, so one day when the seas were moderate we slowed our speed to that of a tanker and pulled alongside. We steamed along about 20-30 feet apart with their fuel lines, supported by booms, stretched over to our tanks. There had to be some meticulous steering or we would have had a major diesel spill all over our deck. The men on the tanker were looking down laughing and joking with our baldheaded crew, most of whom had shaved their heads after the wild scissor-cutting on leaving the US. We were Michael Jordans long before he was born.

Soon we passed within sight of Christmas Island, 1,000 miles south of Hawaii close to the equator. The tropical sun heated up the metal ship and the sleeping quarters became sweaty hot. The breeze through the portholes in the radio shack kept us comfortable at work, but the New Hebrides Islands, the Solomons and the Coral Sea, where we were heading, were going to be hot.

The "shellbacks", sailors who had crossed the equator previously, ordered an initiation ceremony for the pollywogs, those who hadn't, as we crossed into the southern hemisphere. Nobody was exempt, including the officers - all pollywogs. The 20-25 shellbacks set up two rows of 10 men and the pollywogs had to run between the lines and get whacked with pieces of rubber hose or rope. Then each was forced to kneel before King Neptune and be questioned. Nobody knew the answers, of course, so they got rapped on the butt with a loop of rope for each wrong answer, and the ones who had hair left were clipped two inches wide from one ear to the top of the head, then from the forehead to the back of the neck. Pretty soon nearly all the crew were bald as there was no longer any pride in hairdos.

The sonar pinged and the radio crackled as the routine became monotonous. The incessant whine of the diesels rose and fell with the waves as we eased past the islands of Samoa, and a few days later, the Fijis, We had departed San Francisco on August 28, and we reached Espiritu Santo, in the New Hebrides, our active base in the South Pacific, on October 3.

We circled the waters outside the harbor as our freighters filed in and became part of the conglomeration of ships. Then the Tumult and Token sailed in, dropped anchor and cut those droning engines. What a treat to be stable and quiet again.

Sonar Search – Seven Days a Week

Espiritu Santo is 550 miles east of Guadalcanal in the Solomon Islands. The waters in the area are part of the Coral Sea where our navy had fought a vicious battle in May, '42, Our aircraft carrier, Lexington, a destroyer and a tanker were sunk; the Japanese lost an aircraft carrier and a destroyer.

After Pearl Harbor, Japan had captured and fortified islands southeastward across the Pacific with ease - before the USA could muster enough strength to stop them. They had occupied Guadalcanal and were building an airfield there, with great speed, as they were going to make this a major base of operations close to our shipping lanes to Australia. The US could not allow this to happen. So our first order of business in the Pacific was to drive the invaders off Guadalcanal. Thus began the longest continuous battle our country has ever fought. Amphibious forces of navy and marines were dispatched from Australia and Espiritu Santo in early August, 1942 to clear the island, and it took six months.

Japan wanted to keep it, so there was major conflict between the two navies. Five major naval battles were fought along the north shore of the island and so many Japanese and American warships, forty-five, were sunk in this strip of water that it is respectfully referred to as Iron Bottom Sound. And at least half of them are ours as the Japanese fleet was still very strong a few months after Pearl Harbor. Twenty miles north, across the sound was the small island of Tulagi, also well entrenched with Japanese forces. Savo is a tiny island in the middle of the sound. The famous "slot" where John F. Kennedy's PT 109 was sunk is a narrow waterway between the islands to the northwest. The Japanese used the slot at night to ferry more troops to the northwest shore of Guadalcanal.

The heaviest sustained fighting in the Pacific took place in this area and it lasted until February, 1943. The Japanese soldiers fought to the death to hold on, but failed. Twenty-four thousand were killed on Guadalcanal and Tulagi. Twelve thousand were evacuated by Japanese ships as the fighting came to an end. The marines lost 1,800 killed, and thousands wounded, and, the navy, a few thousand in the graveyard of ships in the sound. The airfield the Japanese had constructed was to become Henderson Field, a much-used air base for the US.

Eight months later when we arrived there was a great amount of activity around the airfield and the sound. The enemy were still mad as hornets about losing the island and made an occasional strafing raid with fighter planes on Henderson Field and the ships in Iron Bottom Sound from their huge sea and air base at Rabaul, 600 miles to the northwest at New Britain.

So the Token and Tumult weren't too far from the enemy when we began our "escorting", most of which would be helping to move "stuff" up closer to the action area 400 miles northwest at Bouganville. We were too small and slow to run with the speedy task forces of destroyers and aircraft carriers.

Our job was to travel with slow-moving craft of every description that needed protection against submarines - cargo ships, tugs towing barges or occasionally one of our submarines. On leaving the harbor heading for Japanese waters they would be in danger of being attacked by US ships, so we escorted them, submerged behind our stern, for a day or two until they cleared our shipping lanes.

When we had some time for target practice we fired our guns at sleeves pulled by airplanes or surface raft-targets towed by ships. I am glad we never had to fire at a strafing enemy plane, because I believe we would have missed and it would have killed all of us on the upper deck. Accurately aiming the guns and scoring a hit from the rolling deck seemed unlikely. Our tracer trails (every third was a tracer) were erratic.

The 3-inch gun on the aft deck was 20 feet from us, and I watched the triggerman working furiously trying to focus the gun barrel to fire a shot. The hot, two-foot long empty shell casings that the gun kicked out after a shot were to be caught and tossed overboard by a catcher wearing asbestos gloves, poised behind the gun. Loose casings were soon clanging around the bobbling deck as his scrambling effort to catch them failed. And the noise when all guns were firing was deafening. It is a wonder our hearing wasn't impaired. And one day my 20-mm jammed. One of the 6-inch projectiles was caught in the breech and bent at a 20-degree angle. The shells exploded when the nose hit a firm target and I wondered if the pressure on the nose could have exploded this one. I thought about all these things and how we would fare in the fury of a combat situation with a submarine on the surface or a passing fighter plane. The sub could out-gun us with their 5-inch gun. We would be much better at making depth-bombing runs.

Since the Token was also a minesweeper, we practiced this operation, too, as there would be minefields to clear in the future. We had been "degaussed", a process to make the ship's metal hull immune to magnetic mines in the sweeping process. A 3-inch thick, black electrified cable trailed the ship to explode mines a safe distance away. For conventional mines, two paravanes, small devices like miniature airplanes, were deployed into the water from the bow at the waterline. They pulled cables out on both sides of the bow a hundred feet or so. These cables gliding a few feet under the water would contact the mine's vertical cable and slide it over to the paravane's cutting device at the end. The released mine would pop to the surface where it could be destroyed.

One of our first assignments was to travel with a couple of ships to Guadalcanal. When we completed the trip we were immediately put on patrol of Iron Bottom Sound with our sonar. We got news that the Tumult had arrived a day or two earlier and was now engaged in a bombing run across the sound toward Tulagi. We could hear the muffled explosions, and an oil slick had appeared. They didn't find out if it had come from a submarine or a sunken ship.

We cruised the coast past Henderson Field, up to Savo Island for hours or days until we were given another escort job.

Our hair was growing, and we had settled into general quarters routine twice a day and the around-the-clock work at our jobs. Moore and I were becoming radiomen with respectable ability, and food was good again, if you liked powdered eggs and powdered milk. Our sonar was working 24 hours a day and occasionally we got some pretty firm burps. If the captain and his advisors thought it was serious enough we made a bombing run laying a pattern of seven 300 and 500 pound depth charges ("ash cans") and blew up the ocean behind us. We had to make the run at full speed, 18 knots, as it took them only a few seconds to explode at 100 feet. A 500 was rolled off the stern, a few seconds later, K-guns fired a 300 seventy-five yards off each side, another 500, two more 75's and a third 500, completing the pattern. The explosions vibrated the ship, and a few seconds later plumes of water spewed 30-40 feet into the air. After the water was agitated, sonar was useless for a second run. If a quick pass around the circle revealed no evidence of a hit, and no more burps, we resumed our escort position.

The weeks passed into November and we returned to Espiritu Santo occasionally and mingled with the great ships in the harbor. An aircraft carrier steamed past us and their flight deck soared high above our radar dome on top of the mast. Some of the men were jealous and wanted to transfer to a larger ship. Damaged ships came in - a cruiser with a huge torpedo hole in the side, and a destroyer with 40 feet of its bow missing.

We either dropped anchor or tied up alongside another ship. The crew took turns going ashore for a few hours amidst the mass of men in the flotilla. It was good to step onto solid ground and get a beer with our allotted beer chit. There was a limited choice of things to do - hang out around the landing area or take a hike on one of the two trails through the palm trees. One was a half-mile trek across Aore Island to a beautiful tropical beach and the other, a stroll through gamblers' alley to try to double the money you hadn't been anywhere to spend. Both places were busy. The paradise-like beach was populated with naked sailors running about the sand or swimming from a float 50 yards out in the crystal clear green water. There were a few native huts on the slope overlooking the shore but I never did see any of the locals. The other alley through the palms looked like a contingent of Las Vegas with portable gambling stands set up by entrepreneurs from the fleet lining the path. I am sure there were some professional dealers running these unregulated crapshoots.

The radiomen were able to take a break, as Zaffran would arrange to keep our message log current by getting copies from a nearby ship. We exchanged our movie reels and 78 rpm records with another ship, picked up a month-old bag of mail and slept long hours in the solitude of the harbor. Mail call was attended by everyone and getting news from home was a great morale booster. If we were lucky this vacation would last as long as two days. There seemed to be a great need for sonar escort.

So, one day we were given the task of accompanying a seagoing tug forward from Espiritu Santo to Tulagi. A massive piece of dry-dock equipment was either aboard or astride the barge and it could be seen for miles at sea. Our pace was agonizingly slow as the Token ran a zigzag search pattern ahead of the tug.

On about the third day I was on the morning radio watch when my eyes bugged out as our ship's call letters appeared in a message heading. Pacific Fleet Hq. in Honolulu was transmitting a personal communication to our little ship at sea 3,000 miles away!

Our ship's call letters were NBNS, but were encrypted in the war zone, changing every 24 hours at midnight. Each day the new ones were written in big letters and taped to the typewriter. Fortunately, I recognized them immediately - and was doubly surprised when the big "O", three dashes, meaning urgent, also came up in the heading. I must not make any mistakes!

It was short and sweet - about 25 or 30 code groups. It was over in a minute or two, and had I missed it, no one would have ever known, including me.

I alerted somebody on the bridge that we had received an urgent message. The OD ran in and took it to our decoding machine. There was scurrying about on the bridge a few minutes later when the message was converted to English. It read, "To: USS TOKEN, AM 126 - URGENT - A US NAVY PBY PATROL PLANE REPORTS A JAPANESE SUBMARINE SIGHTED ON THE SURFACE NEAR YOUR POSITION.

Soon our routine for the day was interrupted as the captain ordered everyone to battle stations - for an extended period of time, as we appeared to be an easy target for mischief. We circled the tug and barge the rest of the day and into the night. The next day we were happy that it had apparently by-passed us.

Arriving at Guadalcanal a day or two later we heard that Japanese fighter planes had flown in low over the water from the back side of the island and strafed the ships up and down the coast in Iron Bottom Sound. Two freighters were damaged and beached on the shore near Henderson Field rather than float away with no power. This being our patrol route we felt fortunate to have dodged more than "a" bullet.

We never docked at Guadalcanal during the times we patrolled the bay, but our small boat made trips to shore in connection with our operations there. One day, 2 or 3 miles off shore, we saw something floating in the water and, getting closer, could see that it was the body of a marine, bloated and discolored, in a green fatigue uniform. A boat from shore came and towed it slowly away. This was the only corpse I would see during the war. I can't imagine how this marine lost his life, but I felt for all the thousands who had been killed over there in the jungle and the thousands of sailors entombed in the ships on the ocean floor in the very water we were patrolling. My assignment back at Pleasanton could have sent me to the center of the melee, but I was very content to be on the perimeter, on the Token.

Around the middle of December, '43, we were sent south several hundred miles to New Caledonia, a French Island north of New Zealand. The port of Noumea, a sizeable city, was a beautiful semi-circle of water and beach a few miles across. Quite a number of ships were docked here, and those crewmen going ashore wore dress white uniforms. French was the language of the people and the black police officers wore short pants in the hot summer. The downtown area was bustling with residents and visiting sailors, many of whom were drinking in the "stockade". Not everybody was drinking, however, as it was pointed out that the nice looking residence with the red roof on the hillside overlooking the harbor was busy as a bee, too.

Late in the day, the ships sent their small boats to a pick-up point to retrieve their men gathered around the dock. Most were sober, others staggered around babbling and some of the worst cases had passed out, sprawled around on the sandy beach, drunk on banana rum. When the coxswains identified a man as "one of theirs", they hoisted him aboard. These guys were probably overdue for some fun and diversion.

We celebrated Christmas here and watched a movie on a screen set up on the bow. Dinah Shore was the star. Also, I remember playing poker with a group on the fantail. We were sitting on buckets around a makeshift table. Captain Hudson came and joined the game. We were far enough from the war zone that lights were permitted on deck. But, not for long as next day we were sailing back north.

The radio transmissions from Honolulu took an hour break each morning from 8:00 'til 9:00. During this time the radiomen copied a "plain language" news program sent by Morse code from Los Angeles to keep ourselves posted on world events. We even stayed abreast of what was happening right there in the Coral Sea, Bouganville and the other battle zones in the area as well as the progress of the war around the world. These news articles filled two or three pages, and, we made copies which the crew read with interest. We were in the newspaper business.

January, February and March were just about like October, November and December had been, except at one point we ran through a minefield on entering an unfamiliar harbor. One of our quartermasters had misread a chart. It must have been a magnetic field to which we were immune.

Around dusk one day we were leading a merchant ship away from the coast of Guadalcanal when our sonar gave the strongest signal ever of something 100 feet deep dead ahead. A rush call to general quarters was made and in a matter of minutes depth charges were rolled off the stern and fired off the sides smack over the contact spot. We kept moving as the freighter was close behind and it was too dark to look for evidence of a hit. Our sonar men said, "Now that was a submarine". We could not prove it.

Then came the day in late March as we were approaching Espiritu Santo that Lt. jg. Hensley, our communications officer, asked me to come into his wardroom. He told me the ship had received orders to transfer a 2nd class radioman back to the US for assignment to a "new construction" - newly-built ships needed men with some experience - and they were going to promote me to second class rating and give me the transfer.

What a surprise! Two chevrons and sparks! - equal to the rank of a sergeant in the army. Back to the States and maybe back to North Carolina!

"To The Rear, March!"

Espiritu Santo took on a different aura this time. I wanted to take pictures of this sea of ships but cameras weren't allowed in the war zone. I had my seabag packed by the time we anchored and was hearing "lucky stiff", "good luck" and "have one for me" from friends and radio pals until a motor launch came alongside. I climbed down the ladder into the boat with two or three others going ashore on business. We departed, leaving the Token disappearing in the distance, and I never saw it again. But … 41 years later … a belated surprise!

"American History Illustrated" magazine, to which I subscribed, featured an article in its October, 1985, issue about a diary account of a WWII sailor on the USS Grimes, an assault troop transport, describing the convening of the US Pacific fleet for the first entry into Tokyo Bay in August, 1945, after Japan had surrendered.

It read: "August 25 - Word came yesterday the Japanese peace envoy was cabined with Admiral Halsey aboard the Missouri. Headed in slow, seven knots, today for Sagami Wan, all guns manned and everyone alert for possible Pearl Harbor-type surprises. A minesweeper formation - the Revenge, Token, Tumult, Pochard and ten motor minesweepers - preceded us."

It was exciting, after such a long time, to find out that the ship and crew had survived their 1½ year advance up the Pacific, along with the Tumult, and then had the distinguished experience of clearing the waters ahead of the fleet's victory parade into Japan. These two little ships were better equipped for sea duty than I had originally realized.

Back to Espiritu Santo - 1944. The motor launch landed and I checked into headquarters (hq.) and presented my orders. My assigned living quarters were in a quonset hut among the palm trees up on a beautiful bluff overlooking the harbor. Passage back to the States would be on the Long Island, a medium-sized aircraft carrier used primarily for ferrying airplanes and personnel and it would sail in a few days. I was still ecstatic at my change of direction and didn't care how much time it took. Walking and sleeping on firm ground was a treat. There was roll call each morning and possibly a guard duty assignment for a few hours during the day. Most of the time was free to eat, sleep, read or amble about the area.

My one guard duty assignment was unique. At 11:30 one night a jeep came and took me down to a dock to board a motorboat. Out into the harbor we went into the darkness. We moved among the ships and came alongside a large freighter with a dim light shining way up on the deck. My duty was to take the place of the guard coming down the ladder to the boat. He had been the only human being on the ship and probably was glad to be leaving. I took his 30cal. rifle and went up the ladder. Now I was the only human being on the ship. It was a great lesson in solitude. It was spooky quiet except for creaks and rattles in the rigging and I wondered what in the world could one do, except yell for help, if someone poked his head up over the rail. Rifle shots might cause some ships to jump to battle stations.

So you can see that I kept a wide-eyed watch over the ship during my four hours. When my relief boat came back I asked what cargo was on the ship. The coxswain said it was a load of beer. I didn't ask any more questions.

I enjoyed the R&R for several more days before boarding the San Diego-bound Long Island. They said it was the first of the carriers converted from merchant ships after the war began. The flight decks of these ships, 500 feet, were too short for fighter planes and torpedo bombers, but were great for smaller aircraft on anti-submarine patrol, ferrying planes, etc., and transporting passengers. At 14,000 tons it was much larger than the Token.

We set sail for Honolulu, 3,000 miles away, and it was a pleasure trip for me. I loved the large radio shack. They had a good selection of 78's and we played them incessantly. A radioman named White who had been at sea on a destroyer before the Pearl Harbor attack was just now coming home. He listened to records for hours every day. And we stood watches on the radio to relieve their crewmen a bit.

About a week later we arrived at Pearl Harbor. Our decks were filled with interested viewers as we inched our way into the entrance, turned starboard, through the narrow waters along Ford Island, made a 180 degree turn-around and docked in front of the sunken Arizona. Some of us got our first look at the capsized ships still there from Dec. 7, 1941, and, as soon as we were able to leave the ship, walked the distance back to the Arizona which still had some superstructure showing above the water. A temporary platform had been built above the deck for spectators at this early date - a sorrowful sight.

This would be a four-day stopover for refueling and whatever. The crew not on duty and the passengers were allowed to go ashore each day during daylight hours. So there was a sizeable exodus from the ship early each morning looking for transportation to Honolulu. The early April weather was gorgeous and the city was more gorgeous to all the military men stationed there or in port for a few days. It was abuzz with aircraft. I stood some watches on the radio at night and there were constant voice transmissions from hq., "There are friendly planes in the air", or "There are no friendly planes in the air". So, the state of alert was high.

Waikiki Beach in front of the Royal Hawaiian Hotel was still covered with rolls of barbed wire defenses and sidewalks were crowded with sailors, soldiers and marines looking for excitement and fun. There were crowds surrounding the photo nooks of grass skirted hula-girls taking souvenir shots of servicemen, who loved getting their arms around the girls and their hands in the grass - the girls squealed with delight, and the spectators enjoyed the show. Other skirts got most of the attention - along with the bars which added jocularity to the mix. It was the most spirited atmosphere I had ever witnessed. It was a lot for a 19-year old, who hadn't been around much, to handle, but I enjoyed the parade. However, I did envy those older guys who seemed to be so adept at the ways of the world.

The coastal military cities in the States had the same gung-ho attitude during the war as most people in uniform were highly respected and received the best wishes of the civilian population. Millions of families had a member or relative in the service and our national attention was focused on winning the war.

Five days more at sea and Point Loma beckoned us back to San Diego. The carrier docked across the bay from the Naval Training Station where I had been greeted so rudely 16 months earlier. But I loved the city and wanted to spend more time here. This was not going to happen.

A sheet was posted on the ship giving most of the South Pacific returnees 30 days leave - except most of the radiomen who were cut to 15 days. I had orders to report to Terminal Island in Long Beach, CA, 16 days later. It appeared to be a new ship and a quick return to the South Pacific.

Home, Sweet Home – and a New Ship

I lashed up my seabag again and took the first train to NC. Four days later on a Friday afternoon we were rolling into the western NC mountains. My sister, Julie, was in school at Mars Hill College near Asheville. When we pulled into the station I was utterly surprised to see her standing on the platform to board the train for Smithfield. She was coming home to see me. We had a nice 300-mile visit.

Mother and father were very happy to see me after nearly 1½ years, much of that time not knowing where I was. Braxton was growing up fast and Thomas Carlton (now Tom), in the Navy since Sept., '42, was in the V-12 officer training program and doing well.

One day I walked down the little road to Grandpa's house and Grandmammy cooked a bountiful lunch – including canned peach slices spiced with nutmeg – just for me. This had been a good place to grow up – plenty of space and blue skies.

It was a great morale booster to visit the family and friends. My mother said she had lain awake many nights wondering if I were in danger. All of us were going to church that Sunday morning across the highway, and when she and I walked into Sunday School, a little late, Dad, the superintendent, was talking to the congregation. On seeing us walking up the aisle he choked up and couldn't talk. An assistant finished the proceedings. A number of families had sons in the service.

On my first day at home I had sent a telegram to Terminal Island requesting a 10-day extension in my leave because of the long travel time. Five days later as I was preparing to catch the train, I received a response from the wire. They were giving me five more days. So, after our neighbor gave me some gas stamps (gas was rationed) I resumed visiting all over the place – then, 3,000 more miles on the train. I didn't have any orders waiting for me on arrival back in CA and I wondered if my five extra days had caused a switch in my assignment. But the wait was short.

Submarine chasers were being constructed in Portland, OR, and I was to be the senior radioman on one of these. The navy quarters were small there and we had plenty of time off. A reckless station-bus driver drove us back and forth to the docks where we checked in spare parts for radio equipment to get ready for commissioning. One night we heard the news of the invasion of Europe. It was June 6, 1944.

The ceremony was held on deck with 5 officers and 55 crewmen in attendance. USS PC 795 was a metal submarine chaser (patrol craft) 173 feet long, 18 feet wide and floatable in 9 feet of water. It was much smaller than the Token. The rear deck was 5-6 feet above the waterline. We sailed down the Columbia River to the coast and stopped at Astoria to take on a load of depth bombs. The radio was tuned to a designated coastal station and the sonar put to work as we hit the high seas for San Diego on a shakedown cruise. I had read material about these PC's, which said that, next to a speedy PT boat, this was the roughest riding ship in the navy in rough seas. The long and slim design made the bow rise high over a large wave then dive, with a shudder, into the side of the next one, with the bow under water up to the forward deck-gun. Those of us trying to sleep in the bow section took a 20-30 foot roller coaster pounding. The rear deck was awash at times with waves slopping over the sides. Fortunately, stormy seas were rare in the Pacific. The men on these ships in the North Atlantic must have had a violent ride.

The 20-foot northwest to southeast land swells were giving us a push going down the coast. We lolled over the peaks of the higher waves going our way, and took heavy rolls down into the valleys.

We were soon off the lower California coast where we ran tests on the engines like going from full forward speed to full reverse, a severe test for the engines. We played games with a submarine sent out for us to chase in practice runs and, later, deployed and exploded depth charges to indoctrinate the men assigned to that job. Then we were sent up to Terminal Island at Long Beach for further tests and checks. A few days later we were ordered to San Francisco.

This was a testy trip as our quartermasters couldn't navigate in the impossible fog-bank along the coast. The radio direction finder (RDF) soon found a use as they had to have readings from the stations along the coast to navigate the ship. The RDF was an 18-inch metal loop mounted on a swivel. When the sides of the loop were lined up with the radio signal it indicated from which direction it was coming. So the chief Quartermaster and I had several work sessions in the heavy seas. I gave him a reading from a signal station north, one from the south and one due east on the coast. When he plotted these lines on his chart, perfect readings would show the three lines crossing a single point, otherwise, a small triangle would appear. The center of this triangle was the best guess for our position. The triangles varied in size because of the rough water, but numerous readings kept us off the rocky coast on the two-day blind trip north. At San Francisco we patrolled the outer waters of the Golden Gate.

I began to wonder what plans the Navy had for us. There was talk of our being sent to the Aleutian Islands near Alaska. There were ships of this type used in front of amphibious landings in the South Pacific. Maybe we weren't going to leave the coast. We certainly were enjoying anchoring in the bay and going ashore occasionally. The Navy even sent us out to sea with a fleet of fishing boats. Our sonar was effective locating schools of fish, and the trawlers came in heavily loaded.

One day about a dozen V-12, officer-training students from Berkley, were sent aboard for a half-day patrol - a seagoing experience. Before we left the dock they were full of gusto checking out our sonar, radio, radar and the navigation equipment on the bridge as well as the guns on deck. Their demeanor changed when we passed under the Golden Gate heading for the open sea. The rolling and pitching, plus the salt-spray, soon had them holding on to something or slumped down on the deck feeling bad, and it got worse - most got sick. It was a withered group that bade us goodbye later in the day.

Then came orders to move north to Seattle. This was the roughest time I ever experienced at sea. We were running at full speed against the southward-moving, 25-foot land swells spaced about 100 yards apart - just the right distance to ride high over the crest of one, and slam into the face of the next. This sturdy crew had long ago overcome seasickness, but on this trip at least 25 or 30 admitted to upchucking. We were a day late getting there and some of our metal storage units on the bow were battered.

Our assignment here was to guard the harbor of Seattle where the waters narrow at Port Townsend, 25 miles north. We anchored on the edge of the channel where our sonar could sweep all the way across. Our three radiomen monitored a frequency but we had little communication. We checked in by voice to a shore station on a set schedule.

Weeks and months passed. We spent two days on the ship and one day ashore, if we wanted to go. We rode an ancient bus from Port Townsend to the Port Ludlow ferry which took us to Seattle. Even this easy duty contained a peril which I hadn't thought about. There is a lot of overcast, foggy weather in the area, so foghorns are frequently heard in the distance. I was hanging some laundry on a clothesline on the fantail one night when a blast almost made me drop my wash. I looked up and there was the side of a huge freighter, off course, sweeping by within 20 feet of our ship. We were a sitting duck and could have been sunken right there in the channel.

Our skipper was a 22 year old Lieutenant who had served on PT boats in the South Pacific. He handled this sub chaser as though it were a PT. He liked to approach a dock at a healthy speed, reverse engines heavily and nestle up to the dock. This was scary and sometimes we bumped it a bit. On one occasion we had gone into some backwaters of the Seattle harbor where there was ammunition stored on barges. We probably were going to load on some 3-inch shells or more depth bombs. We were among the barges, approaching one at which a smaller ship was docked with the bow facing us. I was standing on the bow watching the operation and listening to the captain giving orders to be relayed to the engine room. We were approaching at 1/3 speed, which appeared to be too fast, and he yelled out, "Engines back 2/3's!" Somebody goofed and the engines jumped forward 2/3's. Our speed increased and I ran down the deck to jump overboard as he frantically yelled, "All engines back full speed!" The engines grabbed in full reverse, churning up the water, but we jolted the barge and put a dent in the anchor of the other ship.

We occasionally patrolled the Strait of Juan de Fuca out to the coast and on one occasion went to sea off Cape Flattery looking for a Japanese submarine that had been spotted just off the entrance to the harbor. But at Christmas, '44, we were still in Seattle.

Our Communications Officer, Lt. j.g. J.W. Likely from Ohio told me one day that the officer training program, V-12, was going to take 1,500 applications from enlisted men on ships in the fleet for a class convening at Princeton Univ. in the spring of 1945. He said my general classification test score in my service record made me eligible and if I wanted to apply he would recommend me. I told him my brother was already in the program and I would like to apply. He said he would check with 13th Naval District Hq. the next time he was in Seattle. A couple of weeks later he said there was no quota for our group of small ships in the area - but he had applied for a quota. In a few weeks they assigned the group a quota of "one". On this thin thread I submitted my application.

Port Townsend was an adorable little town. Everyone was so friendly. And of course we loved Seattle for the good times we had had there (In 1993, Jane and I drove cross country through the flooded Midwest, along the Oregon Trail route, Jackson Hole and the Columbia River Gorge, on to Portland, Seattle and - Port Townsend. It is a historical attraction now.)

Back To School - OCS

In mid-March '45 I received orders to pack my seabag again. But this time I would be going ashore - to Princeton. I could hardly believe my good fortune and thanked Lt. Likely for his assistance. The first thing I had to do was go into Hq. for a physical examination. I passed this hurdle. So, in the next few days I made some phone calls, said some goodbyes and took the old bus to the Port Ludlow ferry and to Seattle. The train this time would be more comfortable in a Pullman car sleeping in a bed. And I had enough extra days for a return trip to North Carolina. I was enjoying the ride and the scenery through Minnesota when we received word that President Roosevelt had died. It was a shock as he had been a highly regarded leader during the war and had been president since I was 8 years old.

It was good to get home again, and I remember mournful music was played on the radio for days honoring the president. The family were pleased with my new assignment to V-12 - it was on land and not too far from home.

Princeton was an awesome place, challenging one to do well or leave. The campus seemed overrun with Navy as the 1,500 men converged and had to be sorted out and organized. There would be two months of classes, tests and interviews after which only 1,000 would be retained and assigned to the V-12 program. These men had come from ships all over the world bringing all sorts of personalities and egos with them. And it showed. My roommate in 1901 Hall, Gertz from Cleveland, had come from a PT boat squadron in the South Pacific and was the happiest man in the universe to have gotten an assignment to Princeton.

Classes began shortly, taught by Navy officers, in English Grammar, Math, Physics, History and other basic subjects. We received no credits from Princeton, but the Navy used the results to decide which ones to keep in the program. On weekends we were free to roam as we wished. Once a friend and I went to New York - my first visit there. A nightclub in Trenton was another popular hangout. And we had a beer occasionally in the famous colonial fixture on the campus, Nassau Hall, where Revolutionary soldiers also had had one.

One day I was walking downtown when Albert Einstein came out of a shop a short distance in front of me. He looked just like his famous picture with the unruly white hair. He was on the staff in 1945.

The war in Europe came to an end in May, soon after we had begun our studies. Three or four weeks later, military units in the area gathered into a massive formation on the campus parade grounds and speeches were made, with men being called up to receive decorations and awards presented by admirals and generals. It was an impressive ceremony and I felt good being a part of the war-ending celebration. But it was only half over.

Several weeks passed and we were nearing crunch time - would I be one of the 500 rejects?

In late June the survivor's list was posted, and my name was on it. Then a list of colleges and universities conducting V-12 programs with openings for students was posted. There were several in the Northeast, Midwest and Southwest down to Texas on the list, but none in the Southeast, which was disappointing. I wanted UNC or Duke.

Gertz described Baldwin-Wallace University in Cleveland as being a noted private school with great credentials - the pick of the list. Consequently I arrived in Berea, Ohio, on July 4th, '45 to begin some serious bookwork.

"Attention! —- and – Square That Hat!"

The summer of '45 - that sounds like a movie title. And, for me the summer was as serene as a delightful movie. Classical piano music wafted from the conservatory on the campus a block away from main street in Berea. This echoed my feelings exactly as I was elated at having made good, so far, on the opportunity that arose back there on the sub chaser. And now a new door was open and Baldwin-Wallace was an elegant setting to begin work.

We settled into classes, swimming in the lake, and taking the bus to Cleveland on the weekends. It was a long way from the South Pacific and I thought about my friends on the Token. Weeks passed. On Aug. 6 Hiroshima was obliterated by an atom bomb. Aug. 7 was my 21st birthday. On Aug. 9 Nagasaki was blown away and Japan surrendered. The war was over and the world erupted in celebration.

Classes were suspended until the following Monday and everybody joined the hoopla. We were curious as to the future of V-12 now that the military would be demobilizing and discharging millions from the service. But we found there would be no immediate disruption in our program. The celebrating continued as we explored the nightlife of Cleveland. Borsellino's and Alpine Village are a couple I recall. A favorite was the Airways Grill near the airport between Berea and Cleveland. Spirits were sky high and everyone loved servicemen. In September they held a monstrous victory parade and thousands of military men of all branches marched for miles, it seemed, down Euclid Avenue, Cleveland's main thoroughfare, lined with probably a half-million people waving banners and throwing confetti. Our unit of 150 men was in the mix. I was marching in the outside line on the left side, three or four feet from the crowd along the side. The girls would hold handfuls of confetti until they spotted someone they wanted to douse, and then let them have it right in the face. So, our sailors in the outside line got special attention. It was a hoot of a parade.

So, the summer of '45 was a big one in my book and I still have fond memories of Berea and Baldwin-Wallace. We completed a semester and I made some respectable grades, an A and three B's. Little did I realize that a transcript of these grades would be the tool that would get me admitted to the crowded campus of UNC in 1946.

Fall came along and we were then told that V-12 in Berea was being discontinued and our unit would be absorbed into the ROTC program at the Univ. of Michigan.

In late October we bade goodbye to newly made summer of '45 friends and the peaceful setting we had become accustomed to, and moved lock, stock and barrel to Ann Arbor. We were issued white shirts, suit and tie - dress uniforms like Navy officers wore. Nothing was said about the program's being discontinued so we settled down to another semester of work. We enjoyed some football games in the huge stadium and a trip or two to Detroit.

We were well into the term by the Christmas break and our entire family were all present for the first time in years. Tom had been in the V-12 program at Chapel Hill and had received a commission by that time, I think. Julie had come home for the holidays. It was a good post-war visit.

Early in January, '46, the Navy announced their plan for our future - beginning at once. We could continue the ROTC program to graduation and a commission, with agreement to serve 4 years active duty - or sign off now. It was a fabulous offer, but no. They really didn't need us any longer.

My great adventure and experience of a lifetime had only a day or two left to run. And what a trip it had been. Fate had been kind to me.

I packed my seabag for the last time and headed for Norfolk - finally an east coast port.

The Trailways bus stopped at a string of small towns in northeast North Carolina that long day on the way home to Smithfield. I felt adrift - cut loose from the ship. The contentment I had enjoyed belonging to an organization on the move was turning to perplexity as I pondered having to acquire a place to live, income, transportation, food and all the things civilians had to do. I had been laid off - lost my job.

The G-I Bill instituted after the war was one of the most appreciated and beneficial programs our government has ever extended to its citizens. They were giving a big "Thank You" to all who had served the country by saying, "You interrupted your life and education to aid the country, so we will pay for your college degree if you want to go get one."

After The Storm

It had been a struggle for Mom and Dad to operate the farm during the war with insufficient help. So, they decided to rent it to a family with enough manpower to handle it. In Jan., '46, they bought the house that still exists at 702 S. Third St. and moved into town. Mother set to reshaping it to her liking. She soon joined The Woman's Club, both joined the First Baptist Church, and she began practicing in earnest her life-long passion of designing, altering and tailoring clothes. And she did it with class. Over the years many ladies in town brought expensive material to her, to become exquisite suits or dresses. She made numerous wedding gowns with long trains and sequins. She always had wanted to be a clothing designer.

Dad joined the choir along with Mom, also the American Legion and the VFW. They rented the farm for years and finally sold it in 1962. The value had increased 25 times over the 1931 price, so, this money in the bank became some security for their future.

Grandmammy and Grandpa lived on their land until the early 50's, sold the farm and moved into a house near their daughter, Aunt Eva, near Smithfield. Grandpa died quietly at age 86 in Feb., 1953 with Grandmammy sitting by his bed. Then she lived a number of years in the house with Aunt Eva until she died of a hemorrhage at age 88 and was buried on Grandpa's birthday, May 2, 1964.

Tom (Carlton) had continued the Navy V-12 program at UNC and received a commission as Ensign near the end of the war. He was retained in the Naval Reserve and re-called in 1951 to active duty during the Korean War, serving as a supply officer on the aircraft carrier, Midway, in the Mediterranean Sea, reaching the rank of Lieutenant.

After discharge from the Navy in 1945 he remained at UNC for more studies in accounting before taking a job with American Tobacco Co. in Durham. He had met Sara Ellen Joyce, from Winston-Salem, at school and they were married in Oct., 1947. Sally's parents owned a wearing apparel wholesale company in Winston-Salem, D.C. Joyce Wholesale Co., a distributor of Hanes underwear. The family restructured the company with Tom investing and becoming a partner. The new company became Joyce-Munden Co., very successful over the years, and is now Joyce-Munden Sportswear, with Tom still active, along with his son, Tom, Jr., and daughters, Julie Moore and Joy Munden.

I, Jim (Edwin), returned to Smithfield after being discharged in Jan., '46, enrolled in crowded UNC-CH as soon as possible and graduated with a degree, BS-Com. in late '49. I worked in Raleigh until Feb., '51, when I moved to Winston-Salem to join Joyce-Munden Co. I met my dear wife, Jane Daniel, who was secretary of the Junior Chamber of Commerce, and we were married in Oct. '53. We lived in Charlotte for 23 years and our two children, Jim, Jr. and Genevieve, were born there. Jim, Jr., a sound engineer, and his lovely companion, Mary, have a home there. Genevieve works with The Validation Group, currently contracted by Pharmacia Drugs in Kalamazoo, MI. Moving back to Winston-Salem in 1977 I continued with the company, later becoming president, with brother Tom, CEO, to retirement in 1989 - almost 39 years. Tom and I still play a lot of golf together - not too shabbily, either, for our age. But some of my best happiness comes from singing with the angelic choir of St. Paul's Episcopal Church.

Julie had graduated from 12 years in school in Smithfield in 1943 and entered Mars Hill College in the NC mountains. We exchanged letters while I was overseas and she sent me pictures of her friends playing in the snow. It wasn't cold where I was but I loved the pictures. In 1945 she began work with American Tobacco Co. in Durham. While there she met her future husband, Earl Sykes, in 1946 and they were married in 1949. Earl was a foreman in construction work and his assignments took them to some distant and interesting places, over the years, and they had four children while on the move. Tidewater Construction Co. in Norfolk became their main base and they settled there for years. When Earl retired they moved to Palatka, FL where they had been earlier on a project. Jane and I visited them and I played golf a number of times with her, Earl and their power-hitting son, Tommy Sykes, a former ninth-place finisher in the national long-driving contest in Rochester, NY. Tommy's family live there and it is also where Earl and I walked the "ravine" for exercise. Unfortunately Earl died suddenly in 1992, but Julie still lives nearby in Palm Coast with daughter, Kathy, who heads a department in a local branch bank. Sons Earl, Jr., and Buck, and their families live in Norfolk. Julie has been an avid golfer, winning a lot of trophies, and a highly-regarded duplicate bridge player, competing in regional and national tournaments.

Bill (Braxton) had been left alone with Mother and Dad after Julie left home. He was 14 when I left, got an early driver's license at 15, and had become a veteran driver by the time of my visit in 1944. And Dad said he was running the wheels off his newly-acquired '41 Ford V-8. He took me to the Pickwick poolroom in Smithfield and I was amazed at the way he made the cue ball dance around the table. Maybe he liked this better than baseball. He, too, would drive the school bus next school year. He spent some time at Campbell College but I am not sure how long. He served 21 months in the army in late '48 to early '50 turning down an opportunity for officer's training for early discharge. He was discharged one month before the Korean War erupted. .

He took a job in Indiana with The Wrought Iron Range Co. soon after leaving the army. While in the area he met Odell Lynch, his sweet wife-to-be, from Owensboro, KY. They were married and a few years later came to Smithfield with their adorable children, a girl, Terri and son, Jerry, for a visit. Bill had been a sales manager for his firm in the Midwest and was getting ready to go back. Joyce-Munden Co. needed another salesman so he joined the company and moved to Charlotte in 1964 to cover a territory from our branch warehouse there. We visited each other over the years and rode together to many sales meetings in Winston-Salem. Unfortunately, 18 years later he became ill with a brain tumor and passed away at age 54 in 1982. Terri and Jerry have families in Charlotte. Dell still lives at her home there.

Mother and Dad lived on South Third St. for 30 years. All our families visited many times. Dad entered a rest home in 1976 and later moved to one in Kernersville, near Winston-Salem. We visited him often and I was there the evening before he died at 5:00 a.m. the next morning, the day before Thanksgiving, 1982, in a home in Lexington. Bill had died only three months earlier - the youngest and oldest in the family the same year.

Mother had lived at home alone for four years. She was still active and her health was good when she decided to sell the home and move to Winston-Salem near Tom and me in 1980. She lived in an apartment and drove her own car until license renewal time four years later. We saw her often, and she attended our churches and later joined First Presbyterian, Tom and Sally's church. But her health was deteriorating and surgery in 1986 forced her to accept assistance. She entered a rest home, hating it, then passed away peaceably five weeks before her 90th birthday in 1989. A stout heart had come to rest.

On the evening of August 17, 2002, a few weeks ago, when Tom, Julie and I joined our surviving cousins, James, Eula, Grace and Helen at Hopewell Church before the Munden reunion the next day, I asked if anybody wanted to ride over to Pisgah Church. It was still daylight. My daughter, Genevieve, three others and I drove over and parked the car in the churchyard facing the old home place. We talked quietly about the stark chimney standing in a thicket of brush and debris, the house was gone, the two nice pecan trees in the front yard had grown 40 feet high, died and looked like skeletons. The big oak was gone and scrubby trees had grown up in the yard, and a 6-foot fence with a padlocked gate rounded the long curve. Our beautiful farm had become a landfill for the county.

But two things were still in place - Pisgah Church, on our left, and Mr. Breedlove's tombstone beside our car on the right.

Otho and Ila, 1920

Grandpa and old corn crib, 1935

Dad and friend, George, 1922

Market Street, Smithfield, 1927

Munden children, Spring, 1931

Mother and house across from
church, 1937

Cousins Lizzy, Helen, Eula, and
Grace Laughter, 1945

Pisgah Baptist Church, 1936

Grandmammy and Dad, 1960

Edwin, Mother and Carlton, 1940

Statue of Doughboy Soldier - 2003

Grace, Julia, Helen - 1945

Braxton and Mother's concrete walk, 1943

Dad, Braxton, Julia, Jim, Mother 1944

Julia and Mother, 1945

Tom, No. 67, V-12 at UNC-CH, 1945

Jim, ROTC, UM, '45

Tom, 1940

Tom, Pensacola, '42

Jim, Seattle, 1944

Dell, Grandmammy and Dad, 1960

Bill, Dell and Grandmammy, 1960

Sub chaser USS PC795 1944

Jim, V-12, Princeton, 1945

Lt. Tom Munden, USS Midway, 1953

 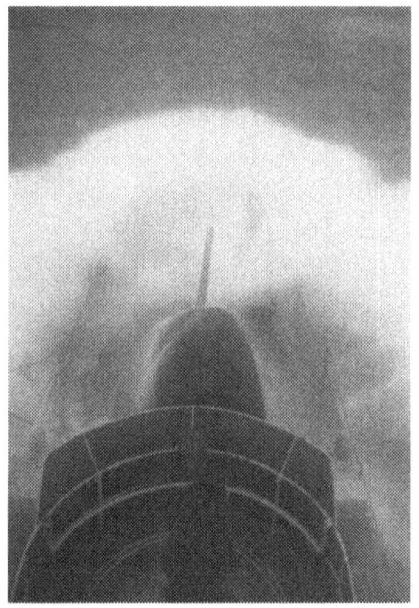

USS PC795 On Patrol 1944
Mild Seas – Jim, 2nd from
left

USS PC795 Heavy Seas, 1944

USS Token – Type Escort Ship / Mine Sweeper 1943

www.ingramcontent.com/pod-product-compliance
Lightning Source LLC
Chambersburg PA
CBHW030343290526
45785CB00004B/1574